Embracing Your True Artist's Destiny

Tending the Flame of Culture

DENI WOHLGEMUTH-PONTY MA, LMFT

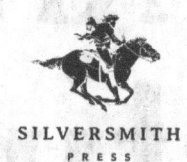

SILVERSMITH
PRESS

Published by Silversmith Press—Houston, Texas
www.silversmithpress.com

Copyright © 2025 Deni Wohlgemuth-Ponty

All rights reserved.

This book, or parts thereof, may not be reproduced in any form or by any means without written permission from the publisher, except for brief passages for purposes of reviews. For more information, contact the publisher at office@publishandgo.com.

The views and opinions expressed herein belong to the author and do not necessarily represent those of the publisher.

ISBN 978-1-961093-99-7 (Softcover Book)
ISBN 978-1-961093-77-5 (eBook)

Dedicated to
Leo and Julia, Walter and Toni

Contents

Introduction vii
Chapter One: You Have What It Takes —*or Do You?* 1
Chapter Two: The Shadow of Van Gogh 9
Chapter Three: Wounding Confirmations: The Hidden
 Treasures of Rejection 13
Chapter Four: Prompted from Within 27
Chapter Five: A Sense of Purpose 42
Chapter Six: What You Have Been Doing All Along 50
Chapter Seven: A Renaissance Here, A Renaissance There 54
Chapter Eight: A Dash for Freedom 63
Chapter Nine: Meeting Up with Destiny 68
Chapter Ten: Poetic Witness – The True Artist Way 79
Chapter Eleven: Van Gogh as Poetic Witness 85
Chapter Twelve: Mastery 90
Chapter Thirteen: The Yoda Principle 100
Chapter Fourteen: A Secret Brotherhood 107
Chapter Fifteen: The Rest of Society 119
Chapter Sixteen: Exile 124
Chapter Seventeen: Genius, Talent, Resentment, Depression 130

Chapter Eighteen: Do True Artists Make Good Art?......................145
Chapter Nineteen: Vision..153
Chapter Twenty: Modern Times and the Language
    of Dreams..155
Chapter Twenty-One: A Messy Divine Order 170
Chapter Twenty-Two: Genius and Mastery 177
Chapter Twenty-Three: Follow Your Passion.................................185
Chapter Twenty-Four: The Attic of Our Life 190
Chapter Twenty-Five: My Father's Piano.......................................198
Chapter Twenty-Six: The Poet of the Two Lines............................207
Chapter Twenty-Seven: Loneliness 226
Chapter Twenty-Eight: Mastery Revisited......................................229
Chapter Twenty-Nine: The Wonderful Wizard of Oz 235
Chapter Thirty: The Practical True Artist 238
Chapter Thirty-One: The Wandering...251
Afterword...257

Introduction

*Art is the queen of all sciences communicating knowledge
to all the generations of the world.*
—Leonardo da Vinci

This book is for you. A book with a title, "*Embracing Your True Artist's Destiny*," appeals only to those who have felt the pull of destiny. You must be one of those. "Destiny" may be a big word, but it merely points to something significant that has a hold on you and will not let you go. It is that something that announces itself forcefully at inconvenient moments when you are all wrapped up in doing things you have decided are "the right things" to do, or it may come in moments of great insight when all at once you see clearly what you are meant for. But then daily life takes over and we dismiss the happy, inspiring moments, or the nagging voice inside as unwelcome distractions or wishful dreams.

I wrote this book to show that these are neither unwanted intrusions nor fanciful imaginings, but serious intimations of your purpose in life. In this book I call them "suggestive hints" that demand to be followed out to their origins, because there you will find the material from which you will build a creative life worthy of the name.

There are already enough "how-to" books and videos on creativity, living as an artist, thinking as an artist, and plenty of books and videos on the making of art, and we do not mean to add to that. There are however, few instructional manuals on "how to be a True Artist," and that is because it is a whole other dimension of the artist life. In this book we dive deep underneath the all-too-common desire felt by many for being creative and artistic (which is a good thing in itself), to a deeper level where we find the almost instinctual urge of a certain type of person. You are most likely one of that type. In every age, in every society, rich or poor, free or unfree, they arise; people like you, whom, in this book, we call "True Artists." They are the ones charged with some inner directive to make sense of the world through making art, and they dignify the human experience with meaning. Their life is about trying to give form to what it means to be alive, to be human, to love, to suffer, to create, to live, with the understanding that we must eventually die. Being a True Artist is not a career choice but a destiny. Going to an art school may help in gaining skill and understanding, however, as a True Artist you must still learn to identify your own path to meaning and unfold it, in your own way, at your own pace. I know this for a fact after having taught for some twenty-five years at art colleges. For the True Artist there are no simple formulas or "recipes for success." If you are a True Artist, you understand this already at some deeper level of your being and did not expect to get it from a book. However, that knowledge, already present, may have gone hidden underneath layers of cultural, familial, and educational conditioning. The question then becomes: "How will you know, and how can you be sure?"

Since the True Artist cannot so easily be categorized or given a clear professional designation, as say, being a lawyer or a doctor, we must approach our subject obliquely, rather than by clear-cut, linear, rational argument. True Artists must struggle to find their proper place in society. This includes many mistakes on the way; false starts, and painful experiences of doubt and questioning, trying on different personae, different approaches, and different strategies. It is a lot of work to get a good fit and find a manner of expression that is congruent with your deepest aspirations. Since your destiny often only slowly dawns on you (even if you are already a working artist), you are often an uneasy fit with those around you, whether they be parents, lovers, or marriage partners. True Artists have a life-long struggle with becoming who they essentially already are.

We approach the material in this book in such a manner that the True Artists amongst us will feel spoken to, will recognize the issues, will know what it is about, will pick up the "hints," and feel "found out" in their hiding places. I say this because most of the True Artists amongst us have been driven into some kind of hiding, irresolute in pursuing their life's purpose, and doubtful about what they have to give or are meant to do. The True Artist may be unsure of what contribution he or she is to make, but that a real contribution is what the True Artist's life is about is felt with passionate certainty.

It is important to understand that by calling someone a True Artist we do not mean to indicate that he or she is a superior kind of artist or a real artist where others are not. We use the word "true" in the same manner as we talk about "true" love. We call something "true love" to distinguish it from other loves. All "loves" are "love," but there is one that is "true." It is true in a way that cannot be denied. Nor can it be explained to someone who has never experienced it; it is known on the deepest level of your being. A woman friend of mine, wise in years, once told me that towards the end of your life, you know who a true love in your life has been, because at that time there is no more denying it. The "true" in True Artist is of that kind.

The True Artist is not about who is the most famous or the most successful, because what constitutes success or fame is too dependent on fashion, differs from period to period and is too dependent on the power players in the field. It is about being "true." This is why some artists are said to be "ahead of their time," which is not so. It is more that they see what their contemporaries do not yet see. They are not so much "ahead" of their time as very much exactly "of" their own time. Others do not see it, but eventually will, exactly because of the work of the True Artist. We will look at that aspect of being an artist in this book from very different angles.

Why are we capitalizing the "T" and the "A" in True Artist? This is merely to indicate that it is a distinction to be taken seriously, and that the True Artist is an important, yes, essential member of society and culture. It is the True Artist who evades the evisceration of the human spirit which political powerplays, and now also an ever-encroaching technology, seem intent on visiting upon us. While power players seem to be manning the societal controls, True Artists are manning controls on a deeper, less obvious level, empowering the human spirit. True Artists "fix" the deep mythological layers of the life of society. They remain therefore beyond the grasp of either the ideological skirmishes of the politics of the day or predatory technological advances. This soft power is their greatness. And their ultimatum.

There is this contemporary dissimulation that "everybody is an artist" or that "anybody can be an artist." The label of "artist" is quickly pinned on anyone who shows some creativity. It must be because we find being an artist a desirable thing to be. This is a rather benign reality, because creativity is indeed desirable, and an essential part of being human. However, being creative is not the same as being a True Artist. And why, we should ask, is being an artist such a desirable thing anyway? Is it because we feel a lack of meaning in our lives? In the well-intended rush to claim the label "artist" for anyone, we have lost our ability to distinguish between the real and the unreal, the true and the pretend.

Sophisticated technology has put abilities at anyone's disposal that had until now only been accessible to a few who spent a lot of their life disciplining their minds and hands. Artificial Intelligence seems to champion creativity, or does it?

The twenty-first century has put its artists in a most challenging situation which we mean to address in these pages. Technology seems to be encroaching on the artist's territory in a big way, and on many other aspects of our lives as well. We feel beleaguered from all sides. This is of natural concern to the True Artist. The encroachment seems to even go so far as on our sense of what it means to be just "human." Artists feel themselves replaced by clever programs, that seem to do with great ease what we always had to learn with great effort. Technological advances seem to be on track to shatter our sense of what it means to be creative. It puts in doubt our sense of being autonomous self-governing individuals, and thus, ultimately, even our right to be here at all. More than ever, we need artists who understand the needs for work on that deeper level. They must have the wherewithal, the creative insight, and technical prowess to restore us to our humanity. And they must do so from the depths of their own true selves, their true humanity, engaging with others at the most significant levels. It is they who will ultimately connect us with each other and our reason for living, and support and protect those most vulnerable parts of us. With all its amazing accomplishments, A.I. brings with it fears that we are being replaced as humans, under the motto of "anything you can do, I can do better."[1] Since we cannot truly understand A.I. and what it means, and recognize, amazingly, that almost nobody out there really does, we are left with dark forebodings that we are strangely becoming superfluous. We feel violated at our deepest level of being human but cannot really put our finger on where nor how. All this is True Artist territory.

What we always thought made us uniquely human seems to be in question and driven into a corner where we feel diminished. We need courageous, deep-going creators who can restore our humanity, away from all that diminishes us and towards the greater poetry of just being alive. They are the ones whom we call True Artists.

Though it seems there are not many things that can avoid the raptor claws of technology, in this book we will find exactly those things that do escape the grasp of technology, the things that technology can *not* do better, cannot invade, or take over. This issue is close to your heart already, otherwise you would not be reading this. By its very nature it seems ephemeral, however, in the face of it, technology stands disarmed! In its blessed elusiveness it is out of reach of technological manipulation. It is good to consider that no matter their proud predictions, the Masters of Technology are not as all-knowing as they like to present themselves. In all their prowess, they are rather overestimated. Ortega Y Gasset, the great Spanish thinker and commentator,

---

[1] Lyrics from the musical "Annie Get Your Gun"—music and lyrics by Irving Berlin

INTRODUCTION

proclaimed in the 1930s,[1] in prescient manner, that our so-called experts, based on their expertise, tend to over-reach. Experts tend to arrogate to themselves knowledge of things that are way outside of their fields of expertise. This is how very smart people can come up with stunningly foolish ideas. They believe, because of their great successes in one field, that they can extend their proficiency to everything else and consider themselves all-around geniuses. This they decidedly are not. That which evades their grasp is exactly what spells the true greatness of the human spirit, and happily, is the domain of the True Artist. It shows that the human spirit may not be reduced to serfdom, even if it may all too easily be seduced into it. One of the most potent affirmations of what it means to be human is wrapped up in the labors of the True Artist. He or she is the one doing the foundational work often hidden underneath the surface layers of life but animating it. This is what makes True Artists "keepers of the flame" and builders of culture.

Our approach to what it means to be a True Artist will be a "wandering," which is a way of advancing while lingering at places that pique our interest along the way. We do not have a GPS destination in mind, and therefore our approach may not appear to be logical, but it will be "psycho-logical," that is, "logical" in a deeper sense. One of the ways I approach some important angles of our subject is by telling you of my own struggles, my own successes, and failures. Because even in this most personal aspect of things, we necessarily land on what is true for all. This is also why we will look at the lives of a few artists who are well-known to you already, and who captured the world's imagination, but whose struggle with destiny may not be as obvious or well-known.

---

1   See his wonderful book "Revolt of the Masses"

The original meaning of the word "destiny" has something to tell us about the meaning of our work: "firming up things, giving definite form to something." Destiny is thus both a firming up and giving form rather than the working out some predetermined reality. The original impulse "to follow our destiny" which launched us on the journey, is the one thing that is a given and not something to be yet formed; it is already in us, awaiting recognition. While the word "destination" is from the word "destiny," for the True Artist, arriving at that destination merely means fully recognizing and embracing his or her destiny.

Often the utter frustration we may feel when on "the path of destiny" is that something in us that knows where it wants to go and somehow knows when it is off course, or still a long way from it; that frustration is a sign of being on the path. A student of mine once confessed that as a young boy already he had this fear of death, and he thought that he was a strange kid because of that. When we had a deep-going conversation about it, we concluded that that fear he felt as a boy was more a first stirring of his destiny in him. That part of him knew that he had not yet built a legacy, had not given form to the deeper stirrings within him. Rather than a neurotic fear of death as such, it was his knowing that his destiny still needed to be formed that appeared as the fear of death; a fear that he may not have time to do it. Thus, from the point of view of the True Artist (and he had proven himself to be just that) his fear came out of his positive and original knowing what needed to be, and the realization that he was far from it; destiny's call was silently operating in him, and in this case was expressed as his fear. Frustration can be a sure sign of our destiny. Destiny is something that awaits our discovery, and our discovery will be in the form of a growing awareness of who we are meant to be, which bit by bit guides our unfoldment. Of course, we do not mean to say that all frustration is a sign of destiny unfolding.

Though we proceed by "suggestive hints," rather than by reasoned arguments, we do need definite things to hold on to and guide us to stay on the path and not go off the deep end. There are two things that ground the True Artist, which are the pillars of the True Artist destiny. These are "mastery" and "poetics." In this book, we will go into some depth about what mastery means, why its pursuit is foundational, and how to approach it and pursue it. Here we will just say that technical proficiency is not the same as mastery, though it is its first stage. The word mastery is used in the wrong way most of the time.

The other foundational pillar that grounds the True Artist, poetics, is more ephemeral, but no less essential and definite. We will see that rightly understood it is quite a solid foundational and something that can be worked on with purpose. By poetics, the art of poetry, we do not mean some intense expression of feeling, or cleverly arranged rhyming words, it is something wider and deeper. It always fascinated the ancient artists, because the essence of a society is in its poetics; people understand it instinctively rather than logically. The True Artist is a true poet because he or she deals in the essentials of life, be it in visuals, music, or language. We will deal with several good examples that make this clear. The art of poetry transforms the inexplicable twists and turns of life into art.

Mastery and poetics are then the foundations on which the True Artist's destiny rests; there is no True Artist without them. We will delve into how mythologies are carriers of these poetic essences, which are part of mastery. We will indicate a simple approach to mythology, which shows that we do not have to become experts in mythology to make it part of our own mastery. Mythology, essentially the stories that society tells itself about itself, cannot but be the domain of the True Artist. Embodied in its narratives are the values and character people identify with. We also have personal mythologies, and we will explore those through my sharing some of my own history. My personal history in itself is not important, but it alone allows me to talk about that part of mastery.

CHAPTER ONE
You Have What It Takes — or Do You?

Correction does much, but encouragement does more.

—Johann Wolfgang von Goethe

How do you know "you have what it takes"? Ultimately, that is what many want to hear from an unassailable authority, or art guru with deep insight into our artistic soul, and beyond. I wanted that so much in my younger years. Some people get to hear this early, but most of us don't. I often wondered how my life might have been different had I heard those words early on, spoken to me with authority by someone I trusted. What I received was often disparaging remarks, and some from an older brother who, when angry with me would blurt out, "You damn little artist!"

What he meant by that I don't know, but what I gleaned was that being an artist was somehow not a good thing! I later realized that there was something else I picked up from his taunting. This would take years for me to understand, and that is the essence of this book.

The last time I saw my mother, she was eighty-nine then, we were talking about all manner of things. Seemingly out of nowhere, she said, "Do you remember when your

CHAPTER ONE

brother would say to you, 'You damn little artist!' I always wondered whether that hurt you at all."

First, I was stunned that she would remember this at all! It took me some time to understand that this was one of her parting gifts to me. We would not meet again after this moment.

In response to her question, I stammered out a dismissive response as if I wanted to avoid the whole question. I said something like, "Oh, yeah, I kind of remember that." I was overcome with emotion. For my entire life that often-used snarling remark resounded in the back of my head. It was one of those things that colors a lot of your life, though you may have forgotten where that color came from. However, I had never brought it up, or discussed it with anyone, convinced that it would have elicited dismissive remarks. I expected anyone who heard me bring this up to accuse me of being immature, saying something to the effect that I should have gotten over that by now. But that my mother thought it important enough to bring up, now that it seemed we might never see each other again, made a deep impression on me. The correct response would have been, "Yes, mom, yes, I do remember it, and it hurt me in a way that I do not fully understand. I am so grateful that you remembered that; now I can let go of it." Hurts like that may seem insignificant, childish even, to the adult in us and to others, but they are significant shapers of our life's path.

It was one of the first times I felt truly acknowledged about being an artist. Others may have said it, but that did not mean the same thing as when I heard it from my own mother, whom I had always loved. It is astonishing to think that my mother brought this up, since I had been a professional artist for many years. I could point to press about my work, and a book of my work published by a British publisher (under a different name!) as a confirmation of being an artist, but that did not rectify the misalignment in my psyche the way my mother bringing this up did. Both my parents—my father had passed some years earlier—had been proud to read about their son in the foreign press, but I could never get a sense of full inner acceptance from their pride in me. How much I had longed for that when I was just an aspiring "damn little artist!"

It is what we all long to hear, but do not get because most of our families of origin have no idea what it means to embrace the life of an artist. If you are lucky, as some of my students were, you are born in a family of artists or art-sensitive intellectuals who understand. But even then, you may not get what you ultimately need to find within yourself: a first glimpse into that specific destiny. The affirmation is very important, and we will get it one way or the other; if we do not, life can be a terrific challenge for those destined to be True Artists. My writing is one way to fully embrace that affirmation for myself. Most of us have no clue on how to do it; it took me a long time to get to it and that was long after I had already embarked on the path. And even when we do, we may feel that we have not done it right!

Another affirmation that was meaningful to me came in a way I still find surprising. It was significant at the time I received it, but it would not gain its full impact until much later, as if it had been a seed planted that had to grow to full fruition later. That is how it is with these things. You may get affirmation, but then the work still needs to be done to allow its full realization whereby it gains full significance.

I first went to college in the Netherlands, where I was born and raised. I studied international business and international relations there. It was quite a beautiful setting; a magnificent castle from the 13th century, complete with

CHAPTER ONE

moat, drawbridge, a rose garden, and gorgeous grounds all around, including a special deer enclosure. However, an art college it certainly was not. Yet, it would prove to be an important station of life for me. I met a very special man there, who gave me what I needed many years later after I had left the school and gone to the US to continue my studies as an exchange student.

Though it was not an art school, it had things that an American student takes for granted but not easily available in my country if at all. Part of the studies were subjects like philosophy, psychology, and lots of language, all of which I loved. While this was part of the curriculum, the usual university education was one of specialization, which meant going to different cities for different specialties. The great smorgasbord selections that an American college offers was just not available. The college was based on the British model, which meant a lot of sports, all-male, and everyone living on campus (now it is co-ed of course). I was a good student but felt out of place. I loved the surroundings though and would take long walks through the beautiful gardens and forest areas with its duck ponds and charming little bridges, which seemed straight out of Monet's paintings. No one else seemed to use the available paths, other than for running training; this amazed me. Because of this sauntering habit of mine, one that I have kept up since then, I earned the nickname, "the philosopher." If you think that was an honorary title you do not know what it is like in an all-male school. It was really meant as a put down. "Damned little philosopher!" would have fit just as well there too.

At the college we would get weekly visits from a minister and a priest (no rabbis). They were there to tend to the souls of the students. The priest had my interest. He was an old man with a long white beard and flowing gray hair. He had seen a lot in his long life and was central casting for a wizard type. He also had a wonderful and infectious boyish laugh, which I remember to this day. He had been a chaplain on the warships in the Indian ocean when the Dutch navy was battling the Japanese in World War II. He had seen a lot of soldiers die and had been there to console and lessen their pain and hardship. He had seen some of the worst of life. He would become very important to me in the years after I had left the college.

When not at the college, he would hold "office hours" at a local hotel for the sailors and marines, with whom he was still very popular, and who would visit him in droves. He was much loved. He also held mass at the chapel in one of the towers of the castle. Hogwarts for real, just on a smaller scale, but no less intriguing.

I visited him many times as I admired his breadth of knowledge, which is, as I learned later, a hallmark of the Jesuits to whom he belonged. I could speak about anything with him. I was not Catholic; he knew that but did not care a whit. Being without a specific religion, I was flirting with agnosticism. I brought him all the existentialist arguments against religion that I had picked up here and there. He would listen patiently and usually knew the arguments better than I did! He would correct my anti-religion arguments, not to counter them, but to make me more rigorous it seemed. By that he taught me more about religion than if he had tried to convert me. In that subdued way of his he taught me an important lesson. He knew the new-fangled atheistic or agnostic theories much more intimately than I did as a19-year-old, yet he was a man of faith and showed me that faith and reason were not antagonistic. That baffled me and more than anything impressed upon me that you can be a discerning intellect and still have faith! He had my admiration.

This man eventually gave me the "you have what it takes" affirmation I had craved more than I was ever able to acknowledge. It came long after I had left college in the Netherlands when I wrote him for his birthday from the US, where I was fashioning an existence for myself. My good friend Bruce, an American exchange student at our college, was better than me at keeping contacts and told me about his birthday. I had been delinquent in keeping in touch with such an excellent man, probably because I felt this need to make a radical break with the past, for reasons only now I can finally understand.

By the time I wrote my birthday card to him, I had decided to pursue art seriously–finally. It is true that I was struggling but I was committed. In my card I wished him a happy birthday and told him that I had fallen away from what I had been educated for and decided to seriously follow the artistic path. To my utter surprise, he wrote me back almost immediately and said, "I have received hundreds of letters for my birthday, but I am going to answer yours first. And I want to say, "You DID it!'" (Actually, for one reason or the other, he wrote it in German, "Es is erreicht!"). He then said, "I always felt that that is what you should be doing, and I still have a painting of yours in my room here." I was overcome with joy since I was in the difficult early phases of establishing an artistic career. "Incredible!" I cried when I read the letter. I consider it a great loss that I lost that letter somewhere in all the moving around I have done over the years. It was confirmation from someone I truly trusted, respected, and admired. That is what I had always wanted, and I got it! Although many years of struggle lay ahead of me, I did get my "You have what it takes!" Without that kind of affirmation, persevering is not so easy. But it is important to see how you can get that confirmation in different and surprising ways, and that it may take many years and much work to finally comprehend the confirmation you always craved and needed. So many moments become fugitive memories, and it is up to each of us to call them back to us if we are to understand them fully.

We must also come to terms with some more challenging "upside down" affirmations. These are the seemingly positive things that turn out to be obstacles to overcome. Being an artist is seen as such a desirable thing in our times that we never stop to think why that would be so. Being an artist seems to stand for truly living, being fully absorbed in one's work, and being carried away by some passion. The portrayal of artists in movies reveals how many of us think about what it means to be an artist. Strangely enough this becomes an obstacle for those we are calling True Artists. They do not seek to model themselves on some faux reality because they want to become aware of their true destiny, which is a lifelong pursuit, and not a romantic fantasy.

We can say that the initial impulse toward being a True Artist is not clear and in fact cannot be. It only becomes so later and then, looking back, you can see that you always had it. The truth is that you cannot move to clarity unless you have that which needs to become clear to begin with. That it can only slowly become clear also means that there is real suffering in it. All those years wondering whether you've "got it" or not, you are actually on a journey to prove it to yourself, and that is an integral part of the True Artist's life-project.

So, you sign up for a glorious battle, though it does not always feel like that. "Get used to it!" an inspiring teacher told me. Yes, you struggle, yes, you get lost, lose track of the

CHAPTER ONE

path, and forget why you are doing this, but then you return, empowered and resolved. Though it may seem that there are those who know from early on exactly what they are meant to be or do, they may miss out on what others (people like me) know who have had to struggle for it. Things which get them back on track whenever things don't go as planned.

CHAPTER TWO
The Shadow of Van Gogh

Great things do not just happen by impulse,
but as a succession of small things, linked together.

—Vincent Van Gogh

Vincent Van Gogh had an uncle, Anton Mauve, who was and is a well-known artist in the Netherlands (Holland), and whose work was popular with collectors. His work was mostly classically inspired Dutch landscapes, a lot of them with sheep grazing in the heather fields with a sheep herder somewhere, or a wonderful depiction of riders on horseback, in high hat and formal clothing, out for a stroll on the beach in Scheveningen (the fishing village and seaside resort I was born in). Pastoral scenes, with farmers and simple folk were some of his favorite themes, and also of the people of Holland. The simple Dutch farmer had the same iconic status in the societal imagination as the cowboy did in the Unites States. And Uncle Anton did them exceedingly well.

After some false starts and failed attempts at doing meaningful work, his nephew Vincent had, finally, decided what to do with his life. He now "knew," at twenty-eight years of age, what he was going to be—an artist, like his uncle. So, Vincent would visit Uncle Anton's studio to ask for advice, and probably receive some professional blessings.

CHAPTER TWO

We can safely say Vincent was a bit neurotic and certainly obsessive. I feel sure that his questions and the nervous energy he brought with him may have disturbed dear Uncle Anton who, judging from his work, preferred quiet over nervous energy. All those questions! Apparently, he was not keen on these visits from his dear nephew Vincent, who now fancied himself to be an artist as well!

When you are in Amsterdam, you will most likely visit the great Rijksmuseum. It is the central depository of some of the greatest works by some of the greatest Dutch masters, especially of the 17th century, known as Holland's Golden Age. Rembrandt's world famous "The Night Watch" is there, and some of Vermeer's works, as well as Frans Hals, and many others; well worth anyone's time. It is a stately building with a very famous library where you can peruse Rembrandt's etchings, the ones he himself pulled from the press, presented to you in a box. You must wear gloves to handle them of course. It is quite an experience to be in that hallowed place and physically handle this great art legacy. The whole building exudes grandeur and houses an important part of the Dutch cultural heritage. The Netherlands lay claim to several world class museums, and this is one of them. Uncle Anton is there too. He has several works in this great collection, small and large; he is part of the great Dutch art legacy.

When you approach the Rijksmuseum from the direction of the great concert hall (where the likes of Mozart and Handel gave concerts), you see a sizable grassy field with the Rijksmuseum in the distance on the other edge of it.[1] But

---

[1] Since 2024 they have been installing a large reflecting pond taking over much of the grassy field. This may be for the unstated reason of preventing large political gatherings forming there, as they did during the covid lock down.

before you get to the hallowed halls of the Dutch masters, a block or so in front of it, is a more contemporary building, which is also a museum. This museum is solely the domain of Uncle Anton Mauve's crazy nephew Vincent. It is the famous Van Gogh Museum. Neurotic, bothersome nephew Vincent has his own museum now, thus outclassing dear Uncle Anton. It is where the largest crowds gather and stand in long lines to be lead in. Vincent got his "you got what it takes!" even if posthumously!

Vincent is loved all over the world. He is what we call a True Artist, the concept that is the core of this book. Individuals from the most divergent cultures feel a special affinity with him; they feel a connection with his work. It is most importantly the work itself, but it is also the story around it. He seems to many people the world over to represent the True Artist, one dedicated to his art alone. We are fascinated by his crazy antics, his suffering, his eventual suicide. We connect with him as someone who was not appreciated by his own contemporaries, by an unfeeling world. Most of us can connect with the sense that the world doesn't seem to care whether we live or die or do great work or not. Vincent is our hero, an anti-hero. In that way he is an inspiration where the successful great artists are not. He cast a long shadow, and as a famous Dutch writer said, "The shadow of Van Gogh hangs over every art exhibit."

This is so because he is also a distraction; a distraction for those of us who are meant to be True Artists. Vincent was a True Artist, but he and his life were also a bit crazy and gives some people the idea that being "a bit crazy" is part of what it takes. The unspoken message seems to be that you can't be "too normal" and still be a True Artist. This is an idea with far reaching consequences, much of it not good.

CHAPTER TWO

This same bad idea can be found in other places. A young jazz musician talking about the great jazz trumpet player Miles Davis showed another aspect of that interpretation which can get the True Artist on the wrong path. Davis was unquestionably a musical genius. His music sounds as fresh and immediate now as it did when he recorded it. The young musician talking about Miles said that he was the one whom most of his musician friends tried to emulate. And then he added, "But usually the only thing they get right about him is his drug habit." Miles was a True Artist, alas, with a debilitating drug habit. Not an addict who could play, but someone who could play, and used drugs. This idea that we can equal the genius of a great artist by adopting his or her bad habits has ruined many lives. Lily Tomlin, the great comedian in her one-woman-show wondered whether "drugs have made us more creative than we really are." This is funny, but also not so funny. Genius does not come from drugs or drink. It comes despite them. How many lives have been ruined by the false ideas, seeing great artists' bad habits and thinking that that is the key to being a True Artist.

Drugs or alcohol can also be used as a palliative for the pain of not knowing for sure whether "you got it." This too, can detour or ruin a True Artist's trajectory. There are also many instances where a successful struggle to free oneself from addiction has become a most powerful way to affirm and invigorate the True Artist destiny. It can get us in contact with the humble dimensions of our being from which creativity flows. It is never the ego's power drive from which great creativity flows. As Carl Jung indicated, it is from the fight with our difficulties that we gain our strengths.

CHAPTER THREE

Wounding Confirmations: The Hidden Treasures of Rejection

Affirmation can come in the form of rejection. Although it is a painful affair, it can be very freeing and eye-opening. In the end it is no less affirming. From my own life I have many such instances. Those are the ones where I gathered strength from the struggle to overcome my initial reaction to rejection, which for many of us tends to come in the form of rejecting the one rejecting us. My own immediate reaction often would be a deep going dejection, a vestige of things that happened in my childhood, and then a defiant, "Well, I'll show you!" type of thing. As soon as I managed to get some distance from the situation, I came to the realization that the intensity of my reaction was actually confirmation of my deep commitment.

I did not have grandparents, and grandparents can play an important role in affirming their grandchildren. There usually is a special bond between them and their children's offspring. My father's parents were victims of the Nazis. My mother barely knew her father who was lost in the first World War, and she did not get along with her mother. My mother's mother died when I was too young to bond with

CHAPTER THREE

her. Where parents may be too adamant about what they want for their children, grandparents often form a gentle counterweight to that.

I had a nice substitute grandmother in my grandmother's sister, with whom my mother got along famously. She did a lot of the things that grandmothers are known for in all parts of the world. She was not married and was the director of a kindergarten and primary school. This sometimes gave a certain authoritative edge to her demeanor, one that could make me defiant, if not openly, then inwardly. But all in all, she was a loving presence and kind towards my brother and me, and that was a stabilizing influence for us, since our home life could often be rather unstable. She was the one who always gave my brother and me sketchbooks and pencils. She was also a wonderful baker, and from her oven emerged the most delicious cookies and apple pies (Dutch apple pie is different from American apple pie; both are great though). I loved her dearly; she went on vacations with us, and I trusted her implicitly. Yet she would be the cause of a deep pain that would awaken me.

She was also the only one I consciously set out to get confirmation from. I wanted someone to tell me, "Yes, you got what it takes," but I did not trust others enough with it. It seems family members are often not the best option here, which I learned the hard way. I chose her because I felt safest with her. So, I planned on getting her feedback on my decision to pursue art as a profession at the right moment. This would have to be when I would be visiting my family in the Netherlands. Phone conversations before cell phones were prohibitively expensive, so we never got to talk while I was away in the far-off United States. It still amazes me that these super long-distance calls are free, and that now you even get to see each other! It is mindboggling for those who did not grow up with it.

By the time I approached my dear substitute grandmother with the grand announcement, I had already been in the US for several years. From much confusion and disappointment, about which I will tell you more later, with much effort I had been able to get a sense of my path in life, which was anything but run of the mill. But at least I knew what I wanted to pursue, well, *needed* to pursue. I was well into my twenties by that time, very much like Van Gogh in that respect.

When visiting her simple apartment where she was living after retiring, at what I thought was the right moment, I made what I felt like my confession. It felt like a confession because I somehow felt guilty about it. This must have been about somehow disappointing the home folks after going off to America to gain a next stage in my education. I was the one lucky enough to be able to pursue a good education and then getting the great opportunity of going abroad, which was seen as a great plus. Of course, going to America was not exactly seen as the place to go to pursue art. But that is what it turned out to be for me. One came to America above all to find a new freedom and to restart one's life according to one's own impulses. That is essentially what I did, though I was not aware of it as such.

My great grand uncle Carl Laemmle had come to America in the early twentieth century for exactly that same reason. America was seen as the land of limitless opportunity, yet it was a much more challenging place for newcomers than when I arrived. No social safety net of any kind, no social services, no special privileges. It was a hard existence for many. But Uncle Carl sure turned out to be a great success, both as a businessman and making a life in art possible

CHAPTER THREE

for many. He would be in fact the creator, not just of his own life, but of the life of millions, by founding Universal Studios. It was he who pioneered the Hollywood studio system as the world has come to know it. He was foremost an astute businessman who saw business opportunities as many others did in that new invention called "the movies." He had a wonderful creative spark and created, together with others like him, a whole new industry and at the same time brought opportunity for so many artists, all drawn like moths to the flame of Hollywood.

Back to my substitute grandmother. She had been a great source of love and remained an important connection with my home country. No matter how radically anti-traditional some people become when they grow up, they somehow remain fond of the special dishes of their youth. One of those is the special food prepared for New Year's celebrations. All societies have their own special foods just for that. They differ greatly from country to country, but they are always an important cultural signifier. Part of important rituals and traditions, they remain significant even for those who pooh-pooh traditions! And my substitute grandmother was one who had always provided some of those Dutch delicacies that are standard for New Year's in the Netherlands. It is interesting to note that these special foods of Dutch culture my substitute grandmother made, found their way to the US via the early Dutch immigrants to New York. They would become America's breakfast favorite: donuts. She would always bring a big bowl filled with these delicious, deep-fried "oliebollen," covered with a kitchen towel. I can still see her from my room upstairs on the third floor in a typical Dutch street, standing before our door with that big bowl that I was eager to dig into on New Year's Eve, dismissing all warnings that it would "spoil my appetite." So, this great aunt was for me the carrier *par excellence* of my Dutch upbringing. She was much more than just a substitute grandmother; she was an important link to my past.

That was why I came to her for blessings on the path I had chosen. It had not been an easy decision, but after a lot of false starts, I knew that now I was beginning to follow my destiny. What I had decided was far removed from what everybody who cared had wanted for me. I was, however, excited about finally being certain, and I wanted her blessings on my decision.

I awaited her response with some trepidation; I felt I had been more direct and open with her than even my parents, who I knew would be somehow critical of my decision. I now realize that at that moment I was up against a mighty fortress wall which is part of Dutch society which I had been slowly breaking down in my years in the US. That wall is a deeply engrained attitude against anything out of the ordinary. It is encapsulated in the oft repeated Dutch saying, "Doe maar gewoon, dan doe je al gek genoeg," which roughly translates as, "Just be normal, that is plenty crazy." Thinking back on it I must have known somewhere deep inside what I would be up against, and this may have been the source of my discomfort. As an aside, this "be normal, that is plenty crazy," somehow coexists with an over-the-top liberalism in a society that quite literally invented modern liberalism. The Netherlands have always been keen on being the frontrunner in the global race towards ultimate liberalism. It seems to miraculously bypass the constraints on what is considered "normal" and what is deemed "crazy." The roots of societal injunctions are deep and mysterious; logical they are not.

Her response was in line with what I understand about Dutch society. In a sweet and gentle way, she said, "Aren't

CHAPTER THREE

you reaching too high?" My feeling response is best described as getting an unexpected punch in the gut. I realize now that I was vulnerable at that point, because despite my "definite decision," I was quite insecure about it. How else could it be? I had to struggle for clarity for so long. The strange thing is that she had always boasted that we had this 18th century Dutch master in the family, good enough to have his work in that fabled Rijksmuseum where the works of Van Gogh's uncle hang as well. Apparently, that was okay, but I was just not in that league in her opinion. I felt that she was telling me that I should not have such a high opinion of myself, imagining that I could compete with "the real artists" out there. She was in fact telling me that I was just ordinary, and that was "plenty crazy." She was right about the "ordinary"—if that is what she meant—but wrong about my being able to hold my own with "real artists." "Ordinary" I consider a plus and a developmental achievement in our narcissistic times!

Having dealt with numerous instances of students asking me whether I thought they "had it" to succeed, I know you cannot give any kind of definitive answer. However we can respond in ways that open the inner resources and strengths of the one asking, which is why they are asking in the first place. It would have been great if my beloved great aunt could have been both confirming and cautionary at the same time. That is very possible, because it is true that to pursue a life in art has challenges that may require inner resources not all of us can easily mobilize. She could have said something like, "You do know, don't you, that you have some family honor to uphold here, so if you are going to do it, I expect you to be serious, do great work, make a contribution to society, become successful, and be happy doing it!" By appealing to the family honor, she might have opened that connection to some unexplored inner resources and infused it with some personal pride. This kind of approach would have appealed to deep roots of belonging and it would have stayed with me and inspired me as a source of strength. Alas, she could not give me that and I felt more alone than ever before. I understand now why she almost had to say it, probably thinking that if she supported me, she might have contributed to my downfall. Yet, I stood up, recovered from the disappointment, and stayed on the path. And that has made "all the difference," as Robert Frost says in his poem. Frost's poem is usually known for the last three lines, but the whole poem is worth our attention in the light of walking the path of destiny we are dealing with here. It is called "The Road not Taken."

> Two roads diverged in a yellow wood,
> And sorry I could not travel both
> And be one traveler, long I stood
> And looked down one as far as I could
> To where it bent in the undergrowth.
>
> Then took the other, as just as fair,
> And having perhaps the better claim,
> Because it was grassy and wanted wear.
> Though as for that the passing there
> Had worn them really about the same,
>
> And both that morning equally lay
> In leaves no step had trodden black.
> Oh, I kept the first for another day!
> Yet knowing how way leads on to way,
> I doubted if I should ever come back.

CHAPTER THREE

> I shall be telling this with a sigh
> Somewhere ages and ages hence:
> Two roads diverged in a wood, and I—
> I took the one less traveled by,
> And that has made all the difference.[1]

I am well aware that many people struggle with worse things in life and may not get any affirmation whatsoever. Compared to them, I was doing well enough. Yet, having only my own life experiences to steer by and to gain a deeper understanding, I resolutely dismiss anyone's effort to devalue or denigrate anyone else's experience of life; this would be in direct contradiction to the task destiny lays on us. Though I do not want to wade into the distasteful morass of moral politics, this is an important point to make. Many are dissuaded from embracing their purpose in life because of a misplaced sense of existential guilt. And as the flight attendant on the plane says, put your own oxygen mask on before you help others. You are of no help if you are unconscious on the floor. To affirm your own life is the first step to empathy with others. To say it rather crudely, you have a right to your own suffering. In a world of tremendous suffering, yes, you have that right! Or, as Carl Jung said, "No tree, it is said, can grow to heaven unless its roots reach down to hell."

I often say that my two cats have a better life than many kids in the world, but does that mean that I should stop caring for them? Or that I should take in all cats I find on the way?

Let's get back to my substitute grandmother and my special connection to her as my only "grandparent." I was

---

1 Robert Frost "The Road Not Taken" – poetryfoundation.org

ready to receive a boost of confirmation from a most trusted source; much needed, because everyone at home was already questioning my strange about-face and turn to art. I had never really chosen for myself any of the other things I had pursued, rather I fell into them by default. But now at least I had chosen! I will explain how that happened because it is worth knowing and can be of help. More about that later.

Still, my substitute granny's refusal brought me face-to-face with what that choice really meant to me, and my resolve deepened, even if it was now a bit less glorious and somewhat shaky, still it revealed new depths. What felt like betrayal actually showed me my own strength of resolve. I did not back off, I went ahead, just an illusion poorer. The pain I felt confirmed to me that I was serious. Later, we will call this kind of approach the "yoga of grief."

Your confirmation may come in the form of something that opposes you. This is how I would relay this kind of insight to my students.

> "When you get blowback, when you are misunderstood, when you get an ultimatum from your family such as, 'You either change direction or we cut off your money,' or when your dreams are being ridiculed, it is God's way of asking you, 'Do you *really* want it?' And if then, despite these seemingly personal disasters, your conviction grows, you are on the path. And it will be less likely that you will ever be thrown off."

Even the universally recognized genius Michelangelo, who has come to us as one of those supremely confident genius types, convinced of his destiny, had much unpleasant blowback to deal with, both from his family, his envious fellow students, and his own struggles with his faith. Calling his own upbringing, "The undeserving nest where I was born," in his sonnets, is a small testimony to that. What we see as the fabled Renaissance, was not that to those who lived it. It is said to be the period from where the whole preoccupation with genius originated, and we would expect from that time a certain reverence towards genius. But Michelangelo's father, a man of standing in the community, was dead set against his son becoming a "lowly" artisan or artist. Michelangelo's instinctual drive and strong sense of his own talent seems to have generated enough personal power to overcome his father's misgivings. He had, according to his compatriots, what Italians call "terribilità"–an often-scary sense of self-assertion, which would make others give way to him. A prodigiously talented individual like him does know that he has "what it takes" to back up that kind of self-assertion, but that does not mean that his inner demons are all conquered; they would plague him for all his life. To the superbly talented it is usually obvious to themselves that they are simply better at doing certain things than their companions, but it does not take away the struggle of confirmation. In fact, the genius type has a very special aloneness to deal with. When we discuss "mastery" in a later chapter we will see that even talent in doing certain things, does not necessarily lead to mastery.

Michelangelo is still considered a prototype of "the genius," and in all the centuries that separate us from him few have come close to matching his achievement. Yet even Michelangelo awakened to his true destiny only gradually. Faster than most, but he was not born fully conscious of it. To think that he is one of those blessed people who never have to struggle with doubt or despair serves more to get us off the hook than to inspire us. It takes moral courage to get out there and work, and find the actual parameters of your talents, rather than spend your life in fantasies of being an unrecognized genius.

The inner call-to-destiny does not tolerate *not* being responded to. Not responding leads to much unhappiness. Therefore, rude awakenings, and I had several, are often a better nudge to follow your destiny than gentle good-natured advice; they are our wounding confirmations. Those rude awakenings are usually more effective because each one presses upon us that though we are quite alone in the struggle even in the best of circumstances, there is this inner necessity, which has been within us all along. A rude awakening pushes us deeper into understanding our own reality demanding to be realized. It is an inner confirmation of a different order.

I was always in awe of the students I had who had that kind of solid intention that I feel I only awakened to piecemeal, and I always wanted to know: Where did you get that? How did you get that? I was truly fascinated by them. I also knew that these students were as diverse as you can get. As their teacher I became increasingly aware that in comparison with the confident talented students, I had always experienced my own struggle for that sense of legitimacy as a life and death struggle. This is not hyperbole; it was that way for me. It may sound dramatic, it may sound over the top, but it was indeed my truth. All our lives are a struggle for meaning and I understood that life would have no meaning unless I responded to my own inner knowing, consequently meeting up with what I knew to be my destiny. For me, it never was happily gliding into an artistic career, it was a struggle, a fight. I began to see that there comes a time when the "art worrier" becomes an "art warrior," willing to fight the necessary battles, without any certainty of victory. That

CHAPTER THREE

is what the warrior does. If I did not follow out my path, it would mean a certain death in life for me; that much I knew. Much later I learned that Carl Jung had said that one of the worst fates that can befall us is a death-in-life. I know what he means by that. I knew I had not much to go on, other than my own inner GPS, faulty as it was, and with no definite destination. Though I took art classes and found some great teachers, I did not know where to go for instruction or information for that other dimension of my search which later I will call "my lowest common denominator," that constant which runs underneath all our struggles. That was what I wanted—needed—most of all. Turns out, I had to make it up, cobble it together as I went along. This was not the time of the Renaissance where you would apprentice yourself to a master and then follow in his footsteps. In our modern times, we are thrown on our own resources and must make our own reality.

The fervent longing to "be an artist" for True Artists is merely the first way that the unfolding path of destiny announces itself. No matter how long that first phase lasts, it is from there forward to an ever-deepening exploration of what it means to stand in the world as such. It is a qualitatively different stance from those for whom making art as a profession is a delightful way to make a living. For the True Artist it is coming to terms with the reality that there really is no other way to be true to oneself than to have a life as a True Artist, fulfilling a mysterious destiny. Being a True Artist is a full-time commitment, with no time off, and no guarantee of success. Some of the aspects of this distinction we will discuss in the chapter on "mastery."

In our times, what we call the "art world" is at a remove from the True Artist. While True Artists may certainly be seen in the "cool" galleries (and hopefully are) that is not their natural destination. True Artists, when recognized, may even begrudge success thrown at them, and resent being a pawn in the art investors' game. The True Artists are the ones who sense what lives deep in the collective mind of society, and who work on bringing about those necessary changes that cannot be brought about either by reason, political action, or ideology. They are the changes that go to the roots of what makes a culture. Societies without culture perish. Therefore, True Artists may be called "essential workers." From their ranks come the pioneers who forge new connections to the intelligence present in the collective mind, obscured as they are by the mad goings on of the world.

My dear old substitute grandmother-aunt's New Year's "donuts" were a delight in themselves, but they were not the road to confirmation. I was alone with something that she could not possibly understand. I, myself, barely could.

There is meaning in what we do spontaneously, instinctively, without thinking, without even being conscious of it. I am not talking about being obsessed with some video game, but of that to which we as kids turn without thinking why we are doing it. In what we do lies a great lesson for us all, and that lesson may also lie in what we fail to do. Sometimes it is because we are talked out of it, or we recoil because of the scrapes it has gotten us into. Eventually the meaning will become clear. The different strands of our life which may seem to be fraying in all different directions will eventually show to have been coming together to become a strong rope by which we may pull our destiny out of hiding and into full focus.

There is a good test to know who is on the path, and therefore refuses to go along to get along, and who is merely obstinate and tries to sell that as a sign of genius. It is the question: do they have "mastery?" Michelangelo may have been difficult to deal with, refusing to adjust to others, but his mastery was beyond most of his contemporaries' level (and he had some very high functioning art contemporaries!), and thus his authority was naturally and firmly established.

What we are calling destiny, some will call your purpose in life. It is the question of "what am I here for?" That is the question to be answered. What we are saying here is that destiny, that purpose, that meaning is already locked up in our psychic being. Some will say it is part of our DNA, though that is hard to prove. These are just different ways of saying that there is something in us that is essential and demands to be brought into full consciousness if we are to live fully. It is something that is most intimately ours yet is at the same time hidden from the "us" we think ourselves to be. This journey of discovery is the most meaningful journey of life. No amount of money or power will satisfy that within us, which is why some very successful people are yet miserable. What I have always known to be the real "me," though at first of necessity only vaguely, took shape only when I got to work. We can look to some artists who have captured the imagination of the world and left us clues, like breadcrumbs to follow home, but ultimately, we must figure it out for ourselves. Such is the burden of modern man. I have always liked what Carl Jung once said about this phenomenon. Jung was a pioneer of the inner realm of consciousness and had many followers who became part of a movement known as "Jungians." At one time he said that he was glad that he was "Jung" and not a "Jungian." His best "followers" were the ones who were able to embrace his approach and come up with their own vision. How can we find our way without merely repeating what was done in the past, or conversely without merely reacting against it?

CHAPTER FOUR
Prompted from Within

> "Everybody experiences far more than he understands,
> yet it is experience rather than understanding,
> that influences behavior."
> —Marshall McLuhan

There was a time when you knew exactly what to do if you wanted to be an artist; the path was rather predictable. You became a painter, a sculptor, a writer, or a musician by receiving the appropriate schooling. You went to an art academy if you wanted to learn the painter's craft, a conservatory if you wanted to be a musician. Even if you had some difficulty choosing between the different arts, things were relatively straight forward. You can see in biographies of famous artists that some had difficulty making that choice. I found an example of that early on in that great biography of Honoré Balzac, written by Stephan Zweig. Balzac, considered one of France's greatest writers, was not sure whether to be a musician or a writer. He is by no means alone.

Then there was this explosion of mass culture upon the earth, and things forever changed and became much less self-evident. What did not change was that there were still those who felt it their purpose, or even passion, in life to become some sort of artist. Some of the choices widened as new creative channels, like moviemaking, opened to the aspiring creative artist. Recently, even more and more channels have been made accessible to any aspiring creator. It is all part of the democratization of art. More access to more people. To become what is rather glibly called a "content creator," a non-specific amorphous term, what is needed is some easily accessible gear like a microphone, a podcast set up, and the talent we call gift-of-gab. What it meant "to be an artist" was something everybody knew somehow. It was evolutionarily determined and carved out, and because of that, it persists in the collective mind. Everyone is, however, also aware that something has changed. This is where it gets interesting for us. It has not really changed for the True Artist, and that is why we must use the designation of "True Artist" to create some order in this explosion that someone called the "everybody-is-an-artist merry-go-round." For the True Artist the path was never clearcut to begin with, and thus its essential character has not changed. Its greatness lies in that it cannot be eroded; it remains by necessity true to itself. Amid all the seemingly consequential and irrevocable changes, it remains what it always was—a challenge for the one so prompted from within.

In all its manifestations, the artist's life always involved developing a definite discipline, a craft, a hands-on know-how to be gathered, a technique to be learned, a method to be thoroughly understood. That reality too has been severely challenged in recent times. Technology opened venues which invited in a large crowd of aspiring creatives, a challenging situation. In the face of that too, the path of the True Artist has not changed, as we will show. For the visual arts, technology seems to have disfigured the path, and art schools are scrambling to catch up with the changing landscape. What do we train our students for? How can we serve those who aspire to what they know to be "an artist," since its evolutionary imprint is within them too, and is not washed away just because of advances in technology. The word "technology" means applied science, the actual stem word being "teknologia," from the Greek, "tekhnë" (art, craft) and "logia," thus meaning basically a systematized craft. This is, once again, where it gets interesting for the True Artist. For the True Artist the path has never been a systematized one, because that would exactly repudiate its very essence. This does not make it easier to talk about, and that is why we have said that the path is indicated more by suggestive hints than by definite directions. This is of course in exact opposition to the tenor of our time, where people even say that they "believe in science," meaning that science has been elevated to religious status. But this has been called "scientism," which is in fact anti-science because true science is exactly the method that is constantly in flux and never definite.

For the True Artist, there is, however, still a path to follow, meandering as it may be.

PSYCHIC ARCHEOLOGY

I can best approach the path opening for us by showing how I experienced it in my own life. I want to use it as one of those suggestive hints we talked about in the beginning. Once I tell you my experiences, I want to go deeper to allow a fuller understanding of what may seem to be experiences of little or no consequence, standard experiences, shared by many. I will do so by approaching them from different perspectives. My work in depth psychology (the psychology of the unconscious) certainly gave me some tools for this kind of work. But there are many ways of approaching it. My own meanderings are hardly interesting, in terms of biographical drama, but they are nonetheless the raw material for my search. They are what I have available to dig into, to unearth meaning, something I call "psychic archeology."

Working with the material of your own life experiences is how your destiny comes into full view and how you gain meaning in your life. Even though knowing about the lives of great artists, as relayed in biographies and videos is helpful and interesting, for the True Artist, it still comes down to exploring–deeply–one's own psyche-archeological site. Our own experiences are like the artifacts dug up by archeologists that allow them to reconstruct the life of which they are the products. That too is the way that we become aware of our own purpose. Some famous artists' lives may be more colorful than ours, but that is not the point. It may make for a better Hollywood movie, but it does not make for a more meaningful exploration of one's True Artist destiny. The fascination with "famous" lives, full of the kind of drama that gets movie makers excited, has no doubt sidetracked many True Artists in their journey of discovering their own true destiny. In comparison to these movie dramas, our own life usually looks rather humdrum and not quite that interesting. But it may be more interesting than we ever dared give ourselves credit for! True Artists must eventually come to know that there is, in their own lives, more than enough material to work with to work out their destiny. It is not the dramatic quality of one's life that matters, it is the quality of meaning we manage to glean from it. Plenty of artists' lives that were uneventful were deeply meaningful. A rather extreme example that is often quoted is the poetess Emily Dickenson (1830–1886). Considered one of America's greatest poets, she lived a particularly uneventful life, solitary and reclusive. With few outer happenings, she mined her life and her mind for ample material yielding truly meaningful work. The German poet Rainer Maria Rilke in his famous "Letters to a Young Poet," (written while he himself was still quite a young poet) gave a wonderful response to an aspiring poet who complained that the environment he grew up in, was thoroughly uninspiring to him as a poet. The complaint was that there was not much to be poetic about in the place he was born and now lived. Rilke responded that if he felt that there was nothing to inspire him, that he should not blame his environment, but himself for not being able to see the poetry in it.

Come along as I explore some of my high school experiences, not because they are extraordinary, but because, while unremarkable in themselves, through them I can show how they proved to be meaningful for my development. You could say that once I was able to see poetry in this rather uninspired environment, it did become remarkable. For many of us, high school is one of those bewildering periods where we go through some of the perplexing changes within ourselves, our bodies, our minds, while all our peers are experiencing similar things, and deal with each in their own ill-equipped ways. Because the changes tend to elicit extreme reactions in some, we often get hurt in ways that stay with us throughout our lives. What happens there stays with us. We certainly fail to see any poetry in it and see it more as the origins of some of our failings in life. We are not capable of a larger or deeper perspective, preoccupied as we are with our own growing pains. In a later chapter we will look upon such concentrated units of meaning in our life as "treasures in the attic of our mind" and high school is certainly a significant collection of such "treasures."

The struggles I faced there were not movie script material (though now I would know how to transform them into

CHAPTER FOUR

dramatic material) but were important for my own inner movie script development. As raw material for our life's work, our high school experiences often stand out, and most often not in terms of the "I peaked in high school" kind of way.

High school presented several major life challenges for me that would take me years to "sort out." At first, I wanted to write "took me years to get over," but in the context of the True Artist existence, you do not need so much to get over it as embrace it and mine it for the meaning it can have for you. When you are a teenager, and your feelings are particularly intense, you can sustain some definite psychic damage it is true. However, now I consider that damage more like sports injuries. If you played football in high school or college you may come out with specific injuries that may plague you for the rest of your life, but they will mostly heal. Later those places where your body was compromised may start to serve as pointers, as hints, to a larger perspective on life and destiny.

Though the educational system that I grew up in was quite rigid, I now appreciate that the teachers in general were quite good; some were experts in their field. I have come to appreciate that they demanded excellence from their students. Though we bristle against these demands as young people, we also have a certain respect for the very enterprise of it, and for the teacher, who is, after all, considered the expert. Sometimes our respect is misplaced, but at that time, the respect was still well earned.

Having coasted through primary school, I thought I would be able to continue that easy going approach to learning in my first year of high school. It worked for a while, and I was put in a newly instituted experimental, accelerated program. This became my undoing; I could not keep up. Today I would have been diagnosed with ADHD, but there was no such diagnosis yet, and I now consider that a blessing. Whatever they threw at me at that time, I could not handle. It was a blow to my self-esteem. I failed and failed spectacularly. I could not understand how that could have happened to "bright, intelligent me," but it did. My self-evaluation was out of touch with reality, and the requirements of a system that was preparing us to take up good positions in society. I was held back for a year, which meant that I had to do the whole class over and was now in the "slow lane" rather than the fast lane. All at once I was one of the supposedly "slow" kids. I felt I had failed my parents, I felt I had failed myself. My mother did not seem as concerned about it, which was puzzling to me, but looking back, I like her for it! She had been a teacher herself and did not seem to take the whole thing in the same way as others seemed to take it. She believed in me in a way that I could not see myself, or if I had seen it, would have thoroughly doubted. Now I knew what it meant to be a failure. This is a great discovery and a gift.

All of us learn that lesson in some way or the other. And it is very valuable. The experience is repeated everywhere around the world in many ways, some more severe than others. But the sense of having failed is common to all and has inner reverberations that stay with us throughout our lives. What we do with the experience is what matters.

The young man I was drew some important conclusions from this experience. Too much of it was destructive, but I also know the productive part of it. The productive part of it was that it woke me up to the necessity of working hard, to really study, to "burn the midnight oil," as they say. And I did. I found I could work hard and that way of approaching things helped me in the early stages of the

CHAPTER FOUR

artist's life, where you must set your own goals and make your own working schedule. But it is also an approach that rides roughshod over the very things that you need as a True Artist. Later, we will call this the "poetics" of life when we discuss mastery. I ran roughshod over many finer instincts that blossomed in my teenage years.

I was determined to salvage my wounded pride, but the classes, other than language studies and history did not interest me much. Alas, I learned to just ignore that part of me that was curious and wanted to know the things I knew were being ignored. So, the young man in me believed that overriding your own insight and interest was part of growing up. I think that was what my mother objected to, because she knew that the rigidity of the system was not for her son. But then, mothers tend to often overvalue their kids. At that time, she may have been the one to hold for me my True Artist destiny that I could not yet grasp for myself.

My road narrowed though when I got to the third year where we had to choose a direction. The options were not great. Either the mathematical side, the "B" track, or the commercial side, the "A" track. Since mathematics are somewhat of a closed world to me, I had to choose for the "A" side, which included bookkeeping and accounting which are even less favorite subjects because numbers easily confounded me. But with my newfound determination I threw myself into it. Getting good grades was now the only game in town. I learned that I could "steel" myself into being successful, follow the rules, and "do the job." It did not give me much of a sense of accomplishment other than knowing that I could be like all the others; but it seemed to make my parents and assorted aunts and uncles happy. I learned that discipline paid off, it makes you respected. Looking back on it, it came at the cost of being cut off from my path of destiny. I cannot say with certainty that it was either good or bad, I just proved to myself that if needed I could harden myself into doing what needed to be done. And it was this ability that eventually allowed me to be in academia for several decades, and that was a worthwhile thing. So, I cannot say for sure whether the whole experience was ultimately good or bad, especially since it did not deter me from my path in the long run. However, it has been an important thing to resolve within myself, no matter how humdrum and uninteresting it may look to others.

Strangely enough for the "A" track students in high school (and "A" does not stand for better, just an indication of the educational track), art was rather unceremoniously cut out. I could never find the reason for it; there seemed to be none. It did tell me this—once you go "commercial," you do not need art. How crazy! That was the one thing I loved doing in that drab, uninspiring school—going up to that luminous art studio on top of the building. It looked like a separate structure as if to crown the old-fashioned design of the school with some kind of glory. The building was forbidding looking, but the studio on top had wonderful light and an exciting amphitheater-style, terraced configuration, where the teacher sat in the middle at the lowest level, while we were grouped around him on three different levels. We had drawing tables and enough supplies. All that was some of my favorite stuff of course, and we were given painting or drawing assignments, though we never got any definite instruction.

Eventually I would receive some actual training at the Royal Academy of Fine and Applied Arts, where I began to attend classes for so-called talented kids on weekends, but in school we did not get it. My high school art teacher was an artist of some renown in the Netherlands and we all saw him as a man of standing. He was gruff and had his own private studio on top of the school as well; such a life, I felt jealous of him! He gave me good grades and would say (since our grades were not letter grades but ranged from 1 to 10), that a "10" was for God, a "9" was for him, and an "8" was for me. His was praise wrapped in a put down as well; and he was good at such put downs. Maybe he had imagined a more exciting life for himself than being a high school art teacher and that made him a bit rough. Later, teaching at college, I taught quite a few high school art teachers, and most were rather happy and nice people, so he may have been somewhat of an exception. I now believe that he probably had an image of himself as a "serious artist" to uphold. He had the required artist's hat on his bald head to prove it.

I tell you all this to get to one of those events, like the unearthed artifacts of the archeologist, shines a light on how life shaped me. After I had already been "banned" as it were from art classes, I had a chance encounter with him that became a significant moment of recognition of my own destiny for me. I already knew then that it was somehow significant, but that was only feeling-wise. Eventually I would have to work like that archeologist, putting the different chards together to see how it all fitted to make a definite object. The initial experience was painful and came in the form of a callous putdown. It remains a most vivid memory. It did not make sense, but it was very hurtful, for no reason, which is the definition of cruel. It happened in one of the little offices of the school assistants and "gatekeepers," on both side of the wide entrance doors. These were two men who kept order in the school, clad in their customary gray working coats, usual in the Netherlands for people behind the scenes. These "assistants" were very good at what they did, they would pick you out of the crowd of students surging in in the morning if you were supposed to be handling some things in an administrative office and had not done so (and boy, did they have an eagle's eye; they knew everyone and remembered your name!). So, one morning I was pulled into one of the assistant's little offices, probably to give me a message to report to some administrator later. This was at the time that I was no longer allowed to have art classes. The art teacher happened to be in this little office as well, and as the assistant was going through some paperwork to hand me, the teacher said something about my no longer being able to come to the studio, a crooked compliment wrapped in rather callous and ultimately cruel language. The hurtfulness of was so obvious that the assistant looked up with a puzzled look, as if to say, "What was *that* all about?" Strangely enough it was a kind of recognition that the teacher saw my being denied access to the studio as too bad, thus telling me that he saw me as special, while at the same time disparaging me for being so. He did it in a way that got the assistant's attention, who looked up from what he was doing with a questioning look that I remember to this day. It was the look of someone who was empathic and could not understand the how and why of what he had just witnessed; he obviously felt for me. You see, that too, in its negativity was, in fact, a recognition of my True Artist self, but presented in a wounding way. Now the task becomes to salvage the recognition from the wounding part and take the gift and reject the rest. That may take some doing!

Thinking back on it now, I can see how that the teacher, who was a dedicated artist, a True Artist, may have seen something in me that he felt a connection with now that I had fallen victim to the system and been "demoted" to the slow students. Maybe it was his way of feeling sorry for me for my demotion. As a teacher you encounter students who

CHAPTER FOUR

have talents or abilities that amaze you. You see a kid who has something special, and they have it naturally and do not seem to know what they got. It may have been that, and the only way for him to acknowledge that was through a put down. This is a bit immature, but I have seen it happen in my teaching experience. That is why I would make it a point to tell students that they should strive to become better than their teacher. This was something that seemed to especially puzzle Asian students—of whom I had many—who had grown up in a system where the teacher was the authority figure not to be questioned.

That episode in that small office was not a pleasant experience, but one that always remained alive in me as both a recognition of and an assault on my integrity. It slumbered in my unconscious, hidden in my mind's attic. It also shows how a kind and empathic witness, here the assistant, can make a difference. I was a sensitive kid no doubt, something I do not like to admit, but which is all too true, and things like that hurt me deeply, and gave me many days, weeks even, of depressive thoughts.

Another one of those woundings, what I now call "bloody blessings," came from my Dutch language teacher. He was the opposite of the teacher that I had had before, who also taught Dutch. He was a literary critic of some renown and he encouraged us to write imaginative essays, which he called "lyrical essays." I did that with gusto; that stuff just flowed out of me, it is close to poetry, and I loved doing it. I may be overvaluing my own talents here, but I do still remember some of the imagery I used then, which was very evocative. It came out of me naturally; it was how I genuinely experienced the world.

The new teacher was stern, strict, unapproachable, and not a very happy man for all I could see. He was one who would give me an underhanded approval notice by humiliating me in class, another "bloody blessing." While handing back our assignments he would be making comments on the work. During his comments on my essay, he took the opportunity to put me down rather sadistically, to the quiet delight of the other students; high school kids are cruel. I had written a "lyrical" essay, which I had been encouraged to do by the former teacher, who appreciated such work. But with this new teacher, the unhappy one, it was about writing "reasoned" essays. The poetic allusions I had made in my essay, were anathema to him. He read them aloud to the class to ridicule them. Then he did it to another kid who was a very good visual artist already, very artistic in many ways, and already put upon because he was so obviously gay. I remember him looking at me with a face deep red with embarrassment and shame and with a pleading sense of camaraderie, as we were both being raked over the coals.

"You will never be able to write a lyrical essay on your final exams," the teacher said in a stern voice, the echo of which I can still hear clearly after all those years. The man will be long gone now, but I carried that snarl within me for many years. The final exam he alluded to was the extensive exam that came upon the conclusion of our four or five years of high school. That exam was something that hung over all of us like a dark cloud; we all knew we had to eventually face it. It was a week of final written exams in literature, accounting, history, French, German, and English, and then some three or four days of oral exams, where we would be questioned on books we were supposed to have read, and in the different languages that the books were written in! No small feat for teenagers. So, this was serious stuff for a young person. Looking back on it, and seeing how education has been dumbed down, I must say that that was a good

CHAPTER FOUR

thing too we had to face. It was a good challenge to a young mind, though the pressure was quite unbearable.

So, this teacher, proclaiming that I would not be able to write a lyrical essay while under the high pressure of the final exams week, had a point. But when he said it, I had a very clear and immediate inner response, "I can do this any time!" And I knew that I could! I can get into that mode of imagining at any time. I am still that way, and it is as true now as it was then. What could this teacher know about that?! But, his cautionary words, his shot across my bow, made me hesitate many a time when I should have just gone boldly ahead.

I learned to write reasoned, logical essays, and I must admit that it has found its proper place, but it was also a wounding that would take many years to overcome. That this memory is still so vivid, means that it is an important event in life. Compared to what some kids face in school right now, it may not seem like much, and it may not be movie script stuff, but that is exactly what we are talking about. The wounding of the True Artist in us *is* a major thing, though it may come in the form of thousand innocuous, small cuts! Those things are always written off as unimportant, but the question should be, compared to what? It is a wounding that only we ourselves can learn to deal with and turn into positive affirmation, because it is never part of a societal class movement. True Artists have no movement to appeal to.

Because of or despite the humiliations of being held back and ending up with the supposed slow kids (nowadays those would get more sympathetic attention) I re-invented myself as a good learner and eventually came in second in my year. Looking back, I realize I paid a heavy price for it. I had little social life to speak of and it certainly put a damper on natural buoyancy. Those things, once made conscious, no longer hurt, but become useful experience and knowledge.

And I learned another lesson there. I was second only to a young woman, very athletic, with bleached-blond hair. She got her bleached blondness from many hours in the swimming pool every day. She was training seriously for the Olympics, and her grades were always better than mine. Yet, she was in the pool each day long before I even got up! The discipline she had in her life, and the scheduling she was required to do, enabled her to use her time more efficiently than I ever was able to do. I have concluded that a lot of athletes in school or college profit from having to discipline their lives. What it takes to become good at their sport spills over into other things they do, and they have a definite purpose in life, even if only for the immediate future. They learn that having a purpose empowers.

CHAPTER FIVE

A Sense of Purpose

Are there ways to get that sense of purpose that young athletes seem to hold even when their contemporaries are running wild? Is there some method that can help us work our way through the cobwebs of doubt and confusion that seem to explode our whole enterprise? Now we want this, then we want that. There is a way, and it is simple and fail-safe. It is one of those open secrets which is seldom practiced because of its simplicity. Some of our challenges are clearly negative obstacles to overcome while others present as negatives then turn out to be positives, even becoming guideposts. We call them "mental attic treasures." But first let us visit a simple method to gain purpose in life when you cannot seem to decide on anything. We will soon see how the True Artist is more a person of destiny, but you cannot become clear on that destiny until you have decided upon something specific. It is just that way. I was introduced to this method by a wonderful businessman I was working for at that time, and he obviously saw a certain potential in me that I could not yet see. He owned a large factory and fashion business, and I was his personal assistant. I grew up in the fashion business, so that was not new to me. Once he asked me, "What are you planning to do with your life?" I could not answer. Maybe if he had been an art teacher, I would have blurted out something having to do with art, but this successful businessman had hired me on the basis of my two degrees in business and he would not have wanted to hear that. In any case I could not tell him that because I was yet unaware of my path; and I had I been I certainly could not have imagined how I could make it my own. Then he taught me something that he declared had made a real difference in his life and assured me it would make a real difference in mine as well.

So, what *was* the purpose of my life? We will speak more about how being a True Artist is not so much about having a purpose as a destiny, but a businessman is about purpose. You can always learn a lot from businesspeople because they live in a world of practical realities, and thus they have something to teach you. Thank heaven I was open to being taught! This man was one in a succession of people I worked with—bosses, teachers, colleagues, and others—who taught me urgent lessons that I needed to learn. I learned that it was important to absorb the lesson and still go your own way. There was a series of people who saw qualities in me that I could not see myself, but whose insights I dismissed, even, or especially, if they were in the form of compliments. So, this man was one in a string of guiding lights appearing on the trajectory of life. For a True Artist though there is a complication which we will have to deal with more throughout.

The method he introduced me to would be very important, though part of my process would prove to be about seeing that it left out things that I knew somehow were important to me in a way few can understand. But what I needed first was a definite direction to my life. The method is simple and direct, as all good advice is. Later, I found this

CHAPTER FIVE

approach stated in different ways, but he was the one who introduced me to it.

When he felt that I was genuinely interested in doing this he asked me to write down everything I had ever wanted to be, to do, to accomplish, and to achieve. "*Write it down!*" he said. It is no good just musing on these things in your head, "*Write it down!*" He told me that he had been told that there is magic in writing things down, and I can honestly say that has proven to be true. I never found a solid reason for it, but it is true. He told me to get back to him once I had accomplished the list. "Don't leave anything out just because it seems too impossible, too childish, or somehow embarrassing," he added, "and don't worry, because I will not insist on you telling me, unless you want to, but *do* it." He advised me to carry a little pocketbook and make notes whenever something that I may have not thought of before entered my mind (the "note" app on your phone does the job, since you have that with you most of the time. But there were no smartphones then). I did that, and it must have been quite an interesting list, and a long one, but alas, I no longer have it to go back to. It was lost in the mists of time.

When I eventually told him that I had the list done, he did not even ask to see it, as I had expected him to do, no matter what he had promised. He just inquired whether it included everything. I could only answer that I thought it did but was not sure. He asked if I wanted more time, and I told him no, because I did not want to prolong the agony. I felt a bit embarrassed, because here I was, supposedly his professional personal assistant, and yet he treated me as if I were his student. The list would also include things that would show that my interests would not align with staying at the company. It is not an easy thing to do, to make a list like that. The voices that arise in opposition to what you are writing down are quite exhausting to deal with. "Who do you think you are?" and "You must be kidding?" or better, "This is so much crap, what are you wasting your time on?" Whatever the voices say, know that this is an important part of doing it. You are calling forth the opposition as it were, the opposition to you being who you are at your deepest level. Some of it sees the light of day for the first time and it is not happy to be all exposed; it feels better as secret longings! In our times we glibly call our purpose our "passion," but passion is a much deeper thing than just an excitement about doing something. The "passion" of a True Artist is a deep, profound, and quiet thing. You cannot have a goal to become a True Artist, but you can purpose to see it more clearly, and that is what this stage is about. First find your purpose than get fancy later.

So, after having drawn out the opposition forces and having them lay their cards on the table so to speak, we get to the next phase. I was expecting a lot, but actually it was rather simple. I only got a "good!" from him when I told him I had done what he had asked. "Now whittle it down to six that you consider the most important ones." I had expected a sort of deep going counseling session, but all I got was, "Get it down to six." Not sure why six, I never asked, but it seemed reasonable enough. But that too was difficult, because when there are a lot of things pulling at you, you do not want to dismiss any of them. It is like letting go of good friends really; you go through a lot of hemming and hawing. What I did not realize then was that all that effort was exactly what was needed to get that purpose out in the open, rather than wrapped up in vague musings, fanciful chatter in the skull. Some of the six seemed blatantly contradictory. Most people spend more time choosing some nice clothes in a store than choosing a career or settling on

CHAPTER FIVE

a purpose. These things are not necessarily the same I found out; it is a different kind of choosing.

I somewhat anticipated the next move I would be asked to make but did not want to face it. Indeed, he directed me next: "Now choose one." *"Oh, no!"* I thought, that is impossible! But eventually I came to understand that it is not the only thing forever and ever, it is the core around which all the other things which are still in play will orbit. These orbits should be seen as elliptical, sometimes close to the one core, sometimes further away. The way this was explained to me toned down some of my misgivings. Yes, I could visualize that—a core with orbiting planets around it, sometimes close, sometimes farther away. I could wrap my mind around that. Now came the clincher though; I was told to be as specific as possible. "The more specific, the surer you are to get what you want!" I was told.

I labored on that for a long time. I thought that being specific meant deciding on an amount of income or a specific place to be, or a definite time frame. And that is indeed what is usually meant by that of course, but that is more for the businesspeople among us. However, all I could come up with trying to be as specific as I could be, was something that really had my heart in it, that I knew deep down as the right thing. It was: "To be a *true* artist." I knew that was all I wanted, and it was clear as day to my mind! That may be too vague for some, but I had done the work as suggested and I had indeed come to a definite conclusion, or at least, definite in the way it was definite for me.

I never told him that of course, because it would show that I did not want to pursue my present position within the company. Looking back, I see that he may have had some plans for me there, including marrying his daughter or something like that. Bless the man, for he made a great contribution to my life, one that I would still like to acknowledge in some way, and by writing it down here, I feel I am, though I must not mention names.

There are several things I learned from writing down and selecting what I wanted with my life. Namely, that I was definitely different in a somewhat disconcerting way! What seemed natural and self-evident for many around me was not so for me. I wasted a lot of years thinking that I had to be more like them. But I learned that in all my supposed "non-specificity," compared to what usually goes for being specific in the world, I had a very specific sense of what I was meant for, though I did not have the wherewithal to name it, nor did I know the form it would take. It is after all not an easy thing to identify. There was no denying that I had come in touch with my core reality, no matter whether it fit in with expectations from the "real world" around me or not. I knew what was real for me, I had plumbed my own depths. It was a lot of work, and the outcome was somewhat disconcerting but undeniable. I really was on this earth for something! But I had no idea how that something was going to work itself out. None. Being a True Artist is not the same as being an athlete, or a businessperson. Yet, now at least I knew what was real for me. And whenever I started to question myself again, as naturally happens when faced with the realities of life, I would only land in the same reasoning I had already engaged in many times in my efforts of making the lists. The same arguments would come up that I had used to come to my conclusions. Through this I gained an inner certainty that no one could take from me. The great benefit of having gone through this exercise is that you have dealt with all the arguments for and against already, faced your demons and whenever you are assailed by doubts (and that happens a lot), the same arguments will come up and

CHAPTER FIVE

you can say, truthfully— been there, done that! Then you are back on the path, no matter how difficult the going is. It is also astonishing to realize how we get back to the same old thoughts over and over again, yet they seem like new thoughts every time.

Let me touch on one of the issues I faced when writing my lists. I wanted to be a musician too, a performing musician. And, I had a hard time letting go of that. I had been playing the guitar all along, it had been my companion through many experiences, and it meant a lot to me. Writing lyrics was also something that I was always doing, while walking on the street, taking the bus, traveling, just lying on the couch. I also had achieved a certain level of proficiency that made people want to listen to me (it is also a great way to woo a desired partner). But I had to admit to myself that I wasn't really that diligent in practicing, and not all that interested in spending all my time learning more and new things. I was happy with a certain level of proficiency that allowed me to make songs. I also had to be honest with myself that I would not want to "pay my dues" by playing in bars or restaurants and do the hard work of finding my bearings in the world of music. Yet, I *am* a musician, and good enough to move an audience, but I have known "true musicians" and I realized that I was not like them. So, I am still a songwriter and love doing it, but I know my limitations. My musical side is one of those planets orbiting around the core of being a True Artist; one concentrated on making visuals with pencils and brushes (or some computer programs now). Music certainly is a part of my "enterprise in life," but that is it—it's part of it—not the core of it!

When you do this exercise seriously, you will get your answer. However, it may not be what you wanted to know, or thought you wanted, but you will know that you have arrived at some of your truth. Dashed hopes are part of finding your path. Sometimes the commitment that results from deciding comes in the form of realizing that you have been doing something all along that you were not conscious of doing. The commitment then comes as an aha!—type moment, where the light goes on and clarifies something that had been present for quite some time, right under your nose as it were, and yet you could not see it. There is some pain in that realization, but it reveals that you are on the path, and then the pain no longer matters.

CHAPTER SIX
What You Have Been Doing All Along

An artist discovers his genius the day he dares not to please.

—André Malraux

When we recently moved into a new house in a different state, I had to decide on what to take and what to get rid of. I eventually decided to take along all my old work that had been partly standing around in the studio and partly hiding in storage. I had not given it that much attention and was tempted to go with the common advice given on wardrobes: if you haven't worn it for a year, get rid of it; but I decided to take it all with me and do the sorting later. Once we arrived at the new home and started unpacking boxes with paintings, I saw work I had done years ago. I was amazed. I now had the insight of someone who had taught art for some twenty-five years and had seen a lot of work from a lot of students. Looking at my own "younger works," I found myself exclaiming, "Not bad at all, not bad at all!" Though I could find fault with much of it on certain levels, overall I realized I had been doing good work, "Right under my own nose" as it were. I had been doing what I was meant to do all along, but I had only regarded it as steppingstones to much greater work yet to come. I had disparaged my own work, probably under the influence of some of the voices of my early years, or those contemporary art currents that I did not fit in with. I had also assembled a head full of supposedly authoritative voices whom I had allowed to set up camp in my head and tell me what I should be doing if I wanted to be counted as an artist. Yet, there was a part of me that was not persuaded and did its own thing regardless. It dawned on me that I had been doing all along what I was somehow still striving for.

André Malraux, the great French thinker, writer, man of action, and even minister in the French government, speaks in his book *"Museum Without Walls"* about how a painter's true voice may start out in a small corner of his earlier work, and then slowly spread over the whole work, eventually making all of it his own. That was a great observation, but I had not quite fully understood it. I first understood it as literally starting out somewhere in a corner of your work, and then taking over the whole surface, but that is not what was meant. What I saw in my own work was that I had mastered certain aspects of the process, color, composition, brushwork, and the thousand little things that go into making art, but the meaning of the work had not been allowed to fully emerge. Learning how to paint was my first and primary step of mastery, but just that, a first step. I may have fancied myself a painter, but that was just the outer layer of the True Artist. I had latched on to a visual language, and a way of handling materials that felt most natural to me. And that was that "corner" of the work that Malraux was talking about. After all, my primary purpose had not been to become a painter, but *specifically* "to be a True Artist!" I had it right from the get-go! I just forgot while fully engaged with gaining proficiency.

CHAPTER SIX

Eventually the light went on, and I was able to see and accept what I had been doing all along but had not been able to wholeheartedly embrace and affirm. That affirmation is the true confirmation you need. This is part of the process of your expertise growing into mastery, which we will take up later. The struggle with the material gives us the excitement of discovery and achievement, but at a certain point you will achieve not just a different level but be in a new dimension. That is the True Artist space.

The obstacles we face become more and more subtle. It is not just with the chosen materials, or so-called "tools of genius," but in the form of career life. There are great opportunities that may advance us but may just as well delay or detour us. "Career advancement," always a desirable for anybody, can be for the True Artist a real challenge. Perhaps this comes in the form of a teaching position at a good art college, like it did for me. All at once the loneliness of the studio is replaced by a vital following of eager students and appreciation by colleagues you sincerely respect. What's not to like? These are all great things, but they may also get us off the path. Why seek out a storm when it is smooth sailing? It has its charms, and we can spend a lifetime in it and feel we are fulfilling our purpose. But for the True Artist, it is not enough.

The True Artist knows he or she is on a life-long trajectory of discovery that requires courage, the courage to change what that famous prayer talks about: "God grant me the serenity to accept the things I cannot change, the courage to change the things I can, and the wisdom to know the difference." The path of discovery, the path of the True Artist, is filled with so many opportunities to exercise that courage. It is always daunting, never easy, and always scary. You are indeed risking something. It is always lonely, because no matter what good advice you may be able to get, it is still your own decision to make, whether to accept things as they are, or move ahead. You will come up against your own limitations, psychologically and technically, with every challenge you take to heart. Even within the process of making a single work, that challenge clearly presents itself.

Your courage will be tested when you start insisting on doing your own work, and you must leave behind all the notions of what you consider great art, and what movements you have championed so far. The great French artist Eugène Delacroix said it best for me: "There comes a time when you have to wipe off all your teachers from the palette." But he also was immersed in the atmosphere of nineteenth century Paris, which meant being enveloped in a sense of striving for great artistic accomplishment. That strikes us now as an enviable atmosphere for creativity to flourish in. In Delacroix's wonderful journals you may find a notation of him having lunch with Chopin and George Sand at his place. Within such an inspirational environment it may be easier to wipe one's teachers from one's palette, as he says. In contrast we feel quite alone and deprived of such an overall climate of excellence. The atmosphere of early Hollywood, with all its accompanying madness, had similar features. Once I was tasked with designing an exhibit on the life of one of its pioneers, Samuel Goldwyn, while working for the Academy of Motion Picture Art and Sciences as their exhibition designer. In the process I got hold of a little notebook that Samuel's wife Francis had kept in which she recorded what they had fed the glittering stars who would attend dinners and luncheons at their home, making sure that they would not repeat the same menu for the same people. The booklet is a who-is-who of Hollywood super stardom, and I immediately connected it with Delacroix's journal entries. Here was a general climate of creativity exploding.

CHAPTER SEVEN
A Renaissance Here, A Renaissance There

This brings us to the observation that there are certain periods in cultural history that have captured the collective imagination, especially of artists. Nineteenth century Paris is one such period. But there is also seventeenth century Holland, a golden age for artists. And the crown jewel of such periods in Western cultural history is the Renaissance in Italy. These "golden ages of art" differ from culture to culture, but some are known all over the world, like the Renaissance and 19th century Paris. When we think of those periods, we feel an acute sense of lack compared to the times we live in. Where is the romance and who are the iconic artists that we would expect in a special place at a special time? It seems that there are times and places that attract or produce great minds and great works, when there seems to be a collective atmosphere conducive to greatness. It seems conditions must be right for the emergence of artistic greatness. China considers its Tang dynasty period (which lasted some five hundred years) as a high point of culture (but the Chinese like to indicate several periods of differing degrees of excellence), while Japan considers the Heian and Edo periods as such. But these did not capture the collective imagination as strongly as did Italy's Renaissance, or Paris in the19th century, and this is not some Eurocentrism at work. Iconic artists of either of these periods are hard ones to get past on your way to doing your own thing. This is so in Asia as well as in the West. We all have a romance with some part of art history, depending on where we are from. While it is likely that some of that love will (and probably should) remain somewhere in your work, it can also become a block to advancing on the road of doing that which you were put here to do. In this, we are alone, at this time of history.

Looking at the fabled Renaissance in Italy, we find a concentrated climate of creativity existing in glittering cities which still have iconic status and have held an appeal for many generations. It birthed the modern fixation with creative genius with a star system of artists. The overall cultural climate somehow produced a stimulating work environment for artists of all sorts. However, for the True Artist, even such a time was one of forging a solitary path. Though the shared religious subject matter was in many ways a sure and immediate path to meaning for any artist, the True Artist was faced with making his or her own way all the same. The prevailing dogma, while allowing a sure path to meaningful work, was also a hard thing to kick against. Only the very best were able to move ahead on that razor's edge. Hence, we see the Greek mythological subject matter appearing in Caravaggio's work, alongside the Christian iconography, and the brazen nudes of Michelangelo (which upset the clergy of the time mightily) behind one of Christianity's main altars in the Sistine Chapel.

Though a certain shared vision existed, it was also a highly competitive environment. That competition brought out the most amazing achievements from its participants, not just in their work but also in the forms their rivalry could take. The wealth and power elite of the time attracted the best artists as a way of displaying their wealth, their power, and cultural significance. Strangely enough the Medici family did not seem that interested in Da Vinci, which may have had to do with his True Artist insistence on following his own star. The endless lists of producers and executive producers we see go by during movie titles, have some of the same intent. Eager to attach their names to great movie projects ("executive producer" can mean almost anything), they do what they must to get their name on the screen.

The kind of concentrated creative atmosphere that we ascribe to the Renaissance in Italy, is what True Artist types long for, and search for, even try to engineer. It is in vain because our age does not have that sense of place that we think we could have found in Paris, or Florence, or Rome. Instagram is a contemporary gathering place of artists, but it is a virtual location, and does not give an actual sense of place. It may be the new place of inspiration, yet it is difficult to gauge. It is impossible to know how or where a new period might blossom again, because it never does so in the same way. I tend to think that it is already breaking upon the world in some hidden place yet unrecognized and championed by those who may be unsure of what they are doing. Despite the technology-driven hyper-connectivity that we live in, the next great thing may yet, and most likely is, being born in obscurity, and may need a long gestation period to break upon the world under the right conditions. True Artists come into the world in congenial as well as in inhospitable times.

It is interesting to contemplate the period of the Renaissance, because behind the surface of our romantic notions about it lies a great reality for us to learn about which is less well known. It was not an easy period to live in, with power struggles erupting all around at any moment. For example, this is why Leonardo da Vinci ended up dying in France. He made the long trek out of Italy, at age sixty-four, packing up everything he had on a few donkeys. France's King Louis the First, had promised him the patronage and protection he so much needed and had lacked in Florence, Milan, and Rome. The not-quite-finished "Mona Lisa" making the long arduous journey on a donkey, wrapped in cloth, is an image pregnant with meaning. Sometimes the most highly prized things come wrapped in lowly cloth.

Strangely, conflict ridden times tend to produce greater art than comfortable times. The Renaissance was such a time. It was itself partly the fallout of power struggles of mammoth proportions between the Christian world and the Muslim world. Though I do not want to argue with the scholars who made the Renaissance their specialty, it is certain that it was major societal conflict which set the Renaissance in motion. Decidedly, it was not a friendly "let us all get creative together" type of atmosphere. Scholars from the great library of Constantinople thought it better to take the great manuscripts in their possession to Italy, to safeguard them against destruction and thus the loss of priceless wisdom. For us living in an information filled world, it is hard to imagine that the works of the great Greek philosophers, Plato, Aristotle, Pythagoras, and many others from whose thoughts and insights flowed much that we take for granted in the modern world, existed often in singular copies. Their existence was almost forgotten and certainly not common knowledge. These priceless works were hastily stuffed into primitive suitcases and taken on a long ship ride to Italy from what is now Istanbul. It is almost impossible for us to imagine the urgency these scholars must have felt to save these manuscripts housed in Constantinople from the sure destruction of the encroaching Ottoman empire, intent on conquering the last bastion of the Eastern Christian empire. The Ottomans had shown their propensity for eradicating the culture of those they conquered, erasing them from history. These scholars knew the fate of such a conquest—their library would be burned, and all would be lost!

What they had feared indeed happened. When the Muslims finally, after several failed attempts, took Constantinople and renamed it Istanbul, they sacked the Christian heritage and burned the library. They took over the Aya Sophia which was the greatest Christian church in the world, placed minarets around it and made it into a mosque.

Those manuscripts, spirited out by concerned scholars and librarians, were the spark of the Renaissance, a rebirth, a re-acquaintance with Greek thought. The fabled Renaissance then was very much a child of world conflict, a bloody blessing on the world. It took a powerful combination of astute minds to make it happen the way it did. The ruler of Florence, Lorenzo de Medici, was a great advocate of culture and gave Florentine culture the many boosts it needed. When the scholars from Constantinople arrived at his doorstep with the priceless manuscripts, he was the one to recognize their importance and had them immediately translated and made available. To this end he set some of the people in his employ to work. Among them was Marsilio Ficino, who was tasked with organizing and translating the great manuscripts brought to their city. Ficino became the heart and soul of the Renaissance, though his name is less well known than that of the Medici family or the great artists who remain to this day synonymous with Renaissance genius—da Vinci, Michelangelo, Raphael, Donatello, Caravaggio, and the like.

This little sojourn into history gives context to our story of culture receptive times, and culture aversive times (like our own). True Artists are born in both, and almost always come into awareness of their destiny through some kind of personal strife. Periods of material ease and comfort do not seem to produce profound art; they may produce novelty and excitement of some sort, or as Mario Vargas-Llosa calls it "a culture of spectacle,"[1] as our own, but they cannot produce what the Renaissance did. Among the saved manuscripts were tracts of high spiritual thought from the ancient world, books collectively known as the Hermetic tradition. The ever curious and interested artists (like Leonardo and Caravaggio, curiosity being a hallmark of the True Artist), became familiar with these works, and this impacted their work and thinking. It became part of the transcendent dimension of their work, a transcendence that before had only been in the context of Catholic teachings, and often hampered by its dogmatism. An enterprise of that magnitude, like the Renaissance, needs a transcendent dimension, otherwise it is not possible. This is how mythological figures like Narcissus, and Bacchus crept into the work of the Renaissance artists like Caravaggio and others. This transcendent aspect may be the greatest thing missing in our times. Politics seems to be our only greater dimension, and that can never fulfill the function of the transcendent, as history has taught us over and over.

It does seem, however, that a neo-Renaissance is brewing. What form it will take is hard to say. It will have to be salvaged from the ruins, the sediments of culture left behind in the wake of the recent technological revolution, and societal upheavals. Hi-tech is produced by smart, highly intelligent but from the standpoint of culture, ultimately mediocre people. We will deal with the ruinous mythology of A.I. and

---

[1] Mario Vargas Llosa. 2012. "Notes on the death of culture." Transl. John King

its anti-dote in another chapter. The True Artist is born in some manner of obscurity. There is this notion that because of our intrusive technology there cannot really be a gestation of the new. This is what is needed for growth, the way seeds are kept in the dark before they can sprout.

Aloneness is part of that dormant darkness, and it is a fertile place, a place of incubation. For True Artists, aloneness turns into solitariness, and this solitude results in their work by way of mastery. Solitariness is the place of creation. I have loved the times that I was part of a creative team and the special energy it generates, but I realize that creativity must come from a place that is guarded and free from the intrusion of togetherness. In an age of smart phones and hyper connectivity, establishing oneself in a productive solitariness becomes part of becoming a master. History's archetypal True Artist Leonardo da Vinci told his fellow artists to be like a mirror, and "absorb everything around you and still remain the same!" That might well be the credo for the True Artist.

By exploring the cultural environment which the Renaissance was to its artists class, and what that may have meant for them, we may be awakened to the importance of supportive surroundings in our own lives, or lack thereof. We are all children of our time and cannot step out of it. Sometimes I believe that the fancy to colonize Mars or the moon, may be an expression of that age old desire to escape one's own times and the mess we made of it. Of course, we could colonize Mars, however we might create the same mess.

The Renaissance was a cultural atmosphere, a psychic current that enveloped all who lived through it, even those struggling near the bottom of the societal ladder. It roused the best talents to produce some of the greatest art ever produced, thus uplifting all. To go to church in one of the magnificent churches built in Florence (especially the famed Duomo by Brunelleschi), and to pass through giant and magnificent bronze doors with some of the most amazing art on it, must have elevated anyone who came through them. This masterpiece was the work of Ghiberti, and when Michelangelo saw these doors, he named them "the Gates of Paradise." Ghiberti had help from other great talents like Donatello and Luca della Robbia, who were part of the genius pool then available.

The Renaissance (roughly the 14th and 15th century) is a case study in how essential knowledge can get lost in the mists of time. It also demonstrates that when it is recovered, it can bring about a most profound inspiration, a boost reverberating through the subsequent ages. It is astonishing to think that the wisdom and achievements of the ancient Greeks, which we now consider common knowledge, had been lost to the world for many centuries. The wisdom that Greeks birthed, changed the world forever. For example, the concept of democracy, a radical innovation in human history, was forgotten and remained hidden and locked up in just a few scrolls and codices, in rare libraries. The Renaissance, so called because it revived the civilizing force the Greeks had unleashed, brought a re-birth of civilizational power. Even today knowledge can get lost. Though we are clogging up our information channels with more and more information, it still can get lost! Now it is not so much a matter of some singular piece of literature lying around somewhere forgotten in a faraway library, but a matter of it being buried under an avalanche of undigested, unchecked, and bogus information rolling over everything like a destructive tsunami rolling over beautifully cultured farmlands, like we saw happening in Japan not too long ago.

CHAPTER SEVEN

Realizing that this can happen and *is* happening, we must come armed with proper perspective.

In search for a proper approach to being a True Artist, many of you have probably already gone through lots of books, videos, lectures, podcasts, TED talks, and whatever is available. You are looking for something that makes sense but seems fugitive, not easily available. More advice is not what is needed; our need is more awareness of what is going on in our own lives as we react to what is going on in the world. We are after a sense of connection, a sense of brotherhood with those who know, and a connection with a deeper wisdom within. This does not mean that we must get all mystical about it. Too much information clogs the system. It is like the undigested food that can poison a body. We are looking for a connection with those who have been where we are, and who keep fighting the fight in their own way. You are certainly not alone; you are however, on your own. That is the nature of the path. To tell you otherwise would be selling you pretty lies.

CHAPTER EIGHT
A Dash for Freedom

When I came to the U.S. as an exchange student and managed to stay on, my deepest intention was to "re-start" my life. In that way I can now see I was following in the path of most of those who came here from the earliest pioneering days. I see clearly how I wanted to discover what my life could be if I started anew as if I had not had the experiences I had had growing up. Of course, this is impossible, which I understand well enough, but it is interesting to me that I was thinking that way. I am about unearthing truths, doing my psychic archeology. I understand that "restart" was the quintessential desire of all those who pulled up their stakes and made the long journey to America, to live in the "New World." Most of their experiences were so much harsher than mine; I had it easy, but on the deeper level of my being, the same drama unfolded. I wanted to "be" as if I had not been who I had been up to that point. I came dressed as an adult, wearing suits as we were supposed to as students in my college in the Netherlands. Then I landed in the midst of hippie culture. The hippie culture had reached the Netherlands as well, but I was never part of it, it all was far away from me. This is strange for me to realize, but it was clarified by some passages in Stephan Zweig's great book, *The World of Yesterday*, where he recounts the beginnings

CHAPTER EIGHT

of both World Wars which he experienced living in Vienna. The Nazis were almost on his doorstep, and yet he did not know about it. There was great unrest in the center of the city, but he had to read about it in the British papers. It was far from him although terribly close by. He learned from this that momentous change can be happening right where you live and yet you may be unaware of it until it spreads to where you live. That is how it was with me and the fabled 60s movement. Amsterdam was a world destination for the hippie crowd and yet all went right past me.

It felt as if I were on some private exodus from an imaginary Egypt of my existence, coming to a sort of "promised land." Yet, my existence had been good in so many ways. I always had enough food, parents who cared for me, a roof over my head, although by today's standards it was quite simple. We didn't have a refrigerator, a washing machine, a shower, a bathtub even, and no television, blessedly.

As a young man growing up on a simple street in The Hague, the seat of government in the Netherlands, I was doing what I thought was expected of me. I tried to fit in. I became more and more estranged from a true sense of self which would lead to having to instigate a radical rupture in my life. This sense of not fitting in is a rather common experience, but again, this book is exactly about those experiences which may seem common but need to be fully realized to create meaning in life.

Coming to the U.S. was for me a dash for freedom. I felt a lot of guilt about it because I felt I was rejecting my upbringing and my parents who were, after all, good people. Only as I grew older could I see how their experiences in the war and afterwards had done untold damage to their lives. In retrospect I can also see how my "escape" was an awkwardly executed embrace of my true destiny. In some of my old notebooks I can see that there was an occasional glimpse of it, but that destiny never came into full consciousness until much later. Now I am so glad I still have most of those notebooks. Mostly I felt lost and alone, wandering from here to there, sometimes following good people, and sometimes falling in with those not so good. The True Artist in me was waiting for the right moment to assert himself. In my psyche-archeological digging, getting in touch with that desperate need I had to start over has been important for me. Just writing it down and giving it some organization for the sake of writing a book, has given much clarity. My life to that point seemed to have been just a preliminary station.

To want to start anew, as if nothing happened growing up, is that not a distinctive feature of a True Artist? To stand in the world as if you had not been in the world before? Yet, to also recognize that there have been others like you, who "made it?" Isn't that the whole enterprise of a True Artist in a nutshell? Are kids not just like that too? They see things for the first time, and it excites them and puzzles them, it frightens them and delights them. Their fight with their upbringing is often an awkward way to assert their right to be here.

I can go into a whole psychological inquiry as to why this young man that I was felt that urgent need to escape his upbringing, his country of origin, and history such as it was. I can find the pathological angles of it all as well, but they do not lead to meaning. Our times tend to "pathologize" everything. More and more, quite natural psychological suffering is seen as a disease of some sort, given a clinical identifier; this seems to be the prevailing wisdom—or foolishness—of our time. I have come to different conclusions. Yes, it baffled me for a long time that I had those strong desires which seemed so different from my fellows, who seemed more "normal" and thus disposed to follow the more well-worn paths in society. Of course, if you want to search for damage in any life, you can find it, but to pathologize life's ups and downs does more damage than whatever damage we may bring to light to explain the reasons for how our life turned out. Many things can go wrong in our lives. There are only two possibilities—they either weaken you, or they strengthen you. There is no middle way. In most cases you have a choice in the matter. Of course, there are certain psychological traumas and mental disorders that take the choice away, but this way of looking at life should not be extended to life in general.

My pressing desire to "re-start" my life was not some pathology, nor the result from psychological damage inflicted on me; it was the pressing need to live according to my own dictates as an artist, pressing to the fore through all the things that had happened in my life. As I said before, I call it "True Artist," to indicate that it is an authentic position in life, a real place in society, a legitimate way of fitting into the life of the community. It certainly is my way of being in the world and it precedes any success in the world. What I suffered from mostly was my yet unformed True Artist destiny. It was a deep promise, and, being yet unfulfilled, the cause of my pain. That unfulfilled destiny was my true pain, not the fact that I may not have been loved in just the right way or that I did not have certain things growing up that others may have had.

There is a difference between making art and being a True Artist. Art making has become synonymous with "expressing yourself." This is a good thing to want to do, but a True Artist sees through this softening of what it means to make art. Not that the True Artist does not want to express him—or herself, but he or she operates from a different set of values in a completely different realm. The True Artist searches for the self but does not see it as a given, in the way people who say "express yourself" mean it. True Artists carry culture forward, and this is larger than the self. In that way they are a different species of creatives. They are the keepers of the flame of culture.

To identify as a True Artist is not a claim to a special status, it is an embrace of the actual nature of the enterprise. It is "true," as we said in the introduction, as some love is "true." Likewise, it is not "true" as in being factual nor, as the dictionary would have it, in the meaning of accurate, but in the meaning of sincere, loyal, dedicated, devoted. It is "true" in that it is unaffected, and without pretension. The life of a True Artist is closer to marriage than to a love affair; it is marriage as extended love. When asked whether he had a love affair with the cello, the great cellist Lynn Harrell answered that indeed that was how it started out, but it then became more of a marriage, as he had grown as an artist.

CHAPTER NINE
Meeting Up with Destiny

You come into your awareness of being a True Artist slowly. For a few, as said, it may be an immediate knowing, an inescapable awareness, but in general knowing who you are as an artist is not an immediate knowing. It is a long process and one never finished. True Artists come into the world somehow equipped for what it is they are meant to be, meant to do, but quite unaware of it except on a very deep and unexplored level. It is not an automatic being; it is a gradual awareness of who they are. The point is to not remain unaware for the rest of our lives. For some the truth of their position in life comes in a flash, a moment of deep insight. For most of us this awareness is composed of many small points collected over the years that come together into an overriding realization. Carl Jung asserts that we "happen to ourselves." As we grow up, we get drawn into all the latest preoccupations of society. The way we think about our lives is influenced by the current of thought we are swept up in, what they indicate with the German word "Zeitgeist," which literally means the "spirit of the times" but wrapped up in one word, which gives it added weight and meaning, impossible to translate.

Modern life, complicated as it is and difficult to be born into, has many ways of distracting us from ourselves, and thus many ways to barricade our natural intuitions behind walls of apparently undeniable verities. Here Marshall McLuhan's observation about thinking is fitting. He says, "There are many people for whom thinking necessarily means identifying with existing trends," which means that few of us have our own thoughts. It feels like we do because after all, the thoughts arise in our own mind, and so we think the thoughts are our own. Yet, they are more the thoughts of the spirit of the times. To step outside of that and into our own thinking, is not easy and becomes more and more challenging, and yet it is our true freedom. It is an essential part of the True Artist path. In our hyper connected world, we are always confronted with other people's thoughts. We quite rightly call many of them "influencers," for that is indeed what they are. They influence our thoughts and steer them in certain directions, determine what we think and even how we think it, although many of them are probably not the wisest of people. We are more like a flock of birds performing amazingly complex patterns in the sky, flying at a specific distance from each other yet without a central command, and each flying in formation.

Making it worse is that we now live in a worldwide culture of addiction. We have addicts running around everywhere, addicted now not just to substances, but addicted to the latest technology, to being entertained, to being sexually stimulated, to being in constant virtual contact, to being given more and more information. This is the contribution of the miraculous smart phone to our lives. This amazing feat of engineering has turned us all into addicts; addicts who usually do not think clearly and are easily led, and easily led astray. The Dutch word for "addict" is "verslaafde," which literally means "enslaved one." While I am very much against overusing the word addiction, it is perfectly

CHAPTER NINE

applicable here. Try to take away a person's smart phone for even a couple of hours and you will see the addict's rage, very much like an alcoholic rage, but one which may be better called "digital-ist rage."

The True Artist always has a fight on his or her hands to escape to freedom; usually an inner freedom, but sometimes it must be an outer freedom as well. It may be a quiet struggle, as it often is, but it is no less of a fight. The very opposition of the world is however also productive of great depth in the work of the True Artist. Getting to the truth of your life goes through many phases, punctuated by poignant sufferings, clues, and warnings, all stages of a growing awareness.

One such stage in my own growing awareness has proven to be of greatest significance. It did not start out very promisingly. It was an unremarkable event, a regular day at the office as it were. At the time I was working in the fashion district in downtown Los Angeles not far from where I would eventually have a wonderful loft studio for many years. But that was years in the future. I was part of a commercial studio turning out fabric designs. This was before the advent of the computer, and so the work was done by hand with paint, gouache, a water-based paint. The work felt rather natural to me. I enjoyed working with paint and was becoming good at handling refined and expensive watercolor brushes. I enjoyed being with a crew of creatives, who were good at what they did and were fun to be around. I became very adept at handling gouache in the process as well. Yet, while I felt somewhat at home in this job, in the back of my head the tape kept running, "What are you doing here? You struggled to get two university degrees, and what are you doing with them, painting fabric designs?" Besides that, the designs were not all that interesting either, since the best-selling ones were usually the less beautiful ones, alas. Though the work itself was nice enough, and I was still young enough to enjoy that, there was that aching question reverberating in my head demanding attention. Looking back, I clearly see that it was the echo of my true destiny, pleading, quite like the nymph Echo in the ancient Greek myth of Narcissus, to be responded to; it was destiny calling. I did not see it that way at the time of course. I just felt a sense of depression while bemoaning my own failure to live up to some inner directive that I was not even sure I had. I also felt guilty about feeling different from my colleagues, who were all good people. They felt my discomfort too. While I got some affirmation out of the work, for at least I was doing creative work, there was something not quite right about it all. Working in the world of commerce with its constant action and energy, has its own appeal though, and can be a good anti-depressant. It can also be a place to get stuck, at least for people like me, saddled with that uncomfortable destiny question in my head.

A True Artist type person has a puzzle to put together. As the pieces of the puzzle fall from the box, they look like nothing that will add up to the picture on the cover of the box. But eventually they will. Alas, the True Artist has all the puzzle pieces, but the box cover image is missing. He or she depends on prompts from elsewhere.

A special prompt which would change the way I made sense of my life, came by way of a verse of only a few lines from a poem. I did not know the title of the poem, nor the name of the poet. Years later, not until search engines became sophisticated enough to make a search quite simple, did I get all that information. I will get back to that in more detail later. I have no idea where I picked up this verse with the few lines; I believe it was in one of those small hole-in-the-wall sandwich stands catering to the fashion workers (the business owners went to restaurants, the workers to lunch stands). This sandwich shop had a rack with assorted pamphlets and small books, an assortment without much consistency, more of an attempt to sell more than just sandwiches. I absentmindedly picked up one of the booklets while waiting for my sandwich, and there somehow my eyes landed on those few lines from a poem, which I could not finish reading because my sandwich was ready. However, by the time I had my sandwich handed to me, my life had changed. The lines I had read became edged in my mind; I felt spoken to on a very deep level of my being.

Only two or four lines was all I could grab from his poem. Simple, yet fateful lines. This is how I remembered them:

"Thank God I am a poet who cobbles shoes, rather than a shoe cobbler who writes poetry."

I immediately understood what the poet was talking about, and that understanding would sustain me through many years of struggle. It did something to me. I knew exactly what was meant, and it was an answer to my inner impasse. I was not just a hapless fabric designer; I was an artist who was "doing fabric designs" to stay afloat in the stream of life. It also was a resounding refutation to all those who had always told me that I did not have to be so serious, and that I could always "do my art on weekends, as a hobby. What's wrong with that?" I always knew deep inside that they did not get it, but it was they who seemed to be on the side of reasonableness, while I only had a vague sense of destiny, which to them was either mere fancy or just plain stubbornness. This poet, however, seemed to understand me. And I understood him as well, and a bond was created between us, one that would deepen over the years as

I learned more about the origins of the poem. I returned to work a changed man.

It took many years before I got to know the poet who had penned those lines for me. By the grace of the increased sophistication of search engines, I found out that his name was Mani Leib (1883-1953), a Russian Jew who had fled from the Soviet Union and come to New York. Where he came from was a part of the then Soviet Union where the life of Jews was very tenuous, and constantly threatened. Now everybody will know the name of that region—Ukraine—but for me this was all obscure information. I only knew about the Soviet Union as an empire. It was the U.S.S.R. when Mani left, a place of oft repeated pogroms. Pogroms were terror attacks by Cossacks who would ride into town on their horses, rape, and massacre everyone they could find and burn the whole place down. Cossacks were and are still known for their virtuoso horsemanship and military prowess. This was a game to them, one of showing who owned the place. There was no rhyme or reason to the attacks. It was a demonic powerplay enacted against a defenseless population of poor Jewish peasants living in what was called a "shtetl," the word for a small village in Yiddish.

Able to somehow escape from there, Leib settled in New York joining its large Jewish immigrant population. He was in heart and soul a poet. To stay alive he was, as is shown from the poem I quoted, a shoe cobbler, repairing shoes for people. As a youth I remember, we still had true craftsmen shoe cobblers, just a block from us. They were expert craftspeople and could repair any shoe, even delicate women's shoes. The workshop was visible from the street through his display window, such as it was, and I can still remember the smell of leather when you walked into the shop. Mani Leib was an expert craftsman, a shoemaker, but his destiny was that of a poet, a True Artist.

Together with some of his literary compatriots and fellow immigrants he started an American Yiddish literary movement, "Di Yunge" (the young ones). New York was a harsh environment, especially in the beginning of the 20th century and not exactly welcoming to poets, least of all ones who wrote in Yiddish. Yiddish is not considered a "high class" language, more of a grab bag language, with words from different languages, mostly German, spoken by the common Jewish people. It is looked upon with scorn by many, even Jews, and yet they will use it from time to time to make a finer point than English would allow them, or to create a connection of familiarity. My father who was not religious at all, and did not see the good of it, would still lapse into some Yiddish words from time to time when he was trying to establish a certain connection with potential or present business associates.

Despite the rampant condescension, Mani Leib and his compatriots were serious about making Yiddish into a "respected" vehicle for poetry. This has been a project of poets throughout the world in different times, as we will see when we take up Mani Leib in more detail. Leib and his fellow authors were, in all their championing of a beloved "lowly language," rather puritan in their art-for-art's-sake approach to their work, motivated by a strong belief in the power of art as a counterweight to suffering, actually more as an alchemical transformation of suffering.

I did not know all this when I came across his poetry in those few lines, yet it was all there, wrapped up in a few simple words of a dedicated True Artist who was reaching out to me across time and space. The message was penned for the likes of me and meant to be received by the likes me, somewhere in time. I realized that, yes, I could do whatever

I wanted or needed to do or be, and yet remain on the path of the True Artist. Whether shoe cobbler, fabric designer or, as later, exhibition designer, story board artist, illustrator, or, yes, even art professor. It had to do with a subtle yet profound change of emphasis. I may not have been as pure minded as Mani Leib, but I knew there was someone in the world who knew me and had spoken to me and given me unshakable strength and staying power. Everything I did from then on was guided by that insight. Thank you Mani Leib! We will return in full to his poem later. In him and his fellow poets the important ideas of American egalitarianism, a concept of culture that was truly new in the world, found passionate expression. They were "marginal" poets writing in the lowly Yiddish language, yet formed their own cultural elite, transforming the lowly into the exalted. This type of enterprise is where the inspiration for a whole culture comes from. This is how True Artists become "culture builders."

TRUTH OF POETRY VERSUS TRUTH OF FACT

Later we will see how "poetics," the poetic dimension of art, is an essential part of mastery, and thus part of the foundation of the True Artist enterprise. The ancient Greek philosopher Aristotle's writings called "The Poetics," has remained the go-to work for artists, writers, script writers, poets, and visual artists. His writings are a deep dive into the poetic dimensions of art. We refer to it here only with a few comments, but want to acknowledge it for the timeless guide it is in our search for our *True Artist's Destiny*. It is likely that it was one of the priceless manuscripts brought to Italy by those scholars from the great library of Constantinople (now Istanbul) fleeing before the invasion that would threaten the library with destruction. Once you become familiar with these "saved" works by Plato, Aristotle, and Pythagoras you will find it hard to imagine that such wisdom might have been forever lost. We live in a time now where everything is stored "in the cloud" never to become lost again (or so we think). For us, getting a copy of one of these priceless works is just a few clicks away on a website.

Aristotle's "The Poetics" is part of what sparked the Renaissance and has remained an authoritative guide for the arts. In a book on this work, S. H. Butcher[1] spells out the essence of what is meant by "poetics." In his commentary he shows us how Aristotle sees the truth of poetry as essentially different from the truth of fact. The poetic mind's special gift is that it can "extract the ore" from the crude mass of facts and "free it from the accidental, the trivial, the irrelevant." In that way, he says, poetry transcends fact. And I like to think that besides transcendence it also digs to the roots of that greater reality in which "facts" are but the surface phenomena.

The poet is the one who takes on the crass facts of life and through a process of transformation, like the alchemists, turns them into inspired meaning. The whole project of the poet is about using everyday language in such a way that it reveals deeper meaning. This is a most apt definition of the True Artist's task as well: to reveal the grandeur hidden in ordinariness. Our lives, ordinary as they may be, are capable of revealing great meaning.

The "poetic" challenges of the True Artist's destiny were made clear to me by the poet Ezra Pound in a poem that reached out to me as did Mani Leib's. Though not in the same manner as the Mani Leib poem, it gave me a certain comfort in my struggles. It provided for the struggling artist

---

1   S. H. Butcher, ed: The Poetics of Aristotle. MacMillan and Co. Ltd

I was a certain gloss of being a "suffering artist," suffering for some truths, and that was something that I needed at the time. It gave a certain distinction to my struggles, a distinction that I had yet to earn. A more critical reaction to the poem developed over the years, but never at the cost of my sense of the light it throws on the path of the True Artist. It is a somewhat harsher, more self-obsessed take than Mani Leib's, but it reached out to me with a power all its own and has remained relevant to me.

Ezra Pound called his poem about the True Artist's path "The Rest," and it identifies many perplexing aspects of the journey we are on.

The Rest

Artists broken against her,
A-stray, lost in the villages,
Mistrusted, spoken-against,

    Lovers of beauty, starved,
    Thwarted with systems,
    Helpless against the control;

    You who can not wear yourselves out
    By persisting to successes,
    You who can only speak,
    Who can not steel yourselves into reiteration;

    You of the finer sense,
    Broken against false knowledge,
    You who can know at first hand,
    Hated, shut in, mistrusted:

CHAPTER NINE

Take thought:
I have weathered the storm,
I have been beaten out my exile.

What this poem said to me at first was simply this: you are not alone, persevere, you are not crazy, the world may be, you may have a certain craziness as well, who knows, but it is not hopeless by any means, and others have gone through the struggle. "Take thought/ I have weathered the storm/ I have beaten out my exile," those were the lines that touched me most of all. And they still do. Yet, after having weathered many storms on the path, I have reconsidered what the poem had to say to me, and realize that certain things in it, though beautifully stated, are not quite appropriate to my own journey. This too is part of the path of a True Artist to becoming more and more authentic, realistically aligning with your destiny and letting go of romantic self-aggrandizement. While I embraced the poem and found solace in it, I also had certain misgivings about it that had to be addressed.

CHAPTER TEN
Poetic Witness – The True Artist Way

Besides suggestive hints, there are also some definitive hallmarks which can indicate the True Artist. There are three basic characteristics—a call of destiny felt deep within, a degree of mastery, and a definite grasp of the poetics of life. This is what makes a True Artist a "poetic witness." Everything is of interest and subject for the work of the True Artist, giving form to what he sees, what she understands, and understands deeply and knows directly. A poetic stance does not mean an other-worldly dreaminess. It means exactly the opposite, since the true poetic vision is one of deeper truth, rather than surface verities. It is said that a great talent can do what others cannot do, while a person of vision can see things that others do not see. The one with vision makes things visible to all. Giving form to what you know, what you see, what you understand, is hard, thus the True Artist must be at home in the trenches of the world, no matter how highly placed he or she may be in terms of worldly accomplishment. The True Artist has a sense of history, of what led up to the times they were born into. There is a sense of camaraderie with those who have gone before and fought the same fight for clarity. To the True Artist, the news is not anything new, but a page of history. Yes, it may feel that the world of our own times is going off the rails, but it has been doing so for as long as we have historical records. Those people who say that "this time it is different" have been with us forever as well. Yes, "but this time it *really* is different!" they will exclaim. The collapse of the world has been prophesied from the beginning of history. Da Vinci dealt with those deep-rooted anxieties in the human spirit in some of his later drawings of a flood and seems to have been doing so by means of his own feelings. That is exactly a True Artist at work. Not trying to lecture us or make grand pronouncements but showing things through the work they do. Da Vinci brings us the experience of a scary crescendo of some approaching cataclysm. He does it, not by sounding an alarm bell or issuing a stern warning or giving ideological explanations, but by means of something he loved so much and was fascinated by all his life: the patterns described by the flow of water. Because he had studied it so deeply, so obsessively, all his life, he could produce it from within himself. He could make us experience the agitation of the sea in a simple drawing. It was a storm brewing; he gave it form from within. He was not a dispassionate outside observer and commentator; he produced from within.

Images of flooding or tidal waves occurring in our dreams often point to the deep unconscious flooding the ego self. At the same time, it is an actual construct outside of ourselves, a natural phenomenon in nature. But Da Vinci connects what lives in him with something within all of us by means of his mastery, that coming together of his superb skills with insights from his deeper self. Together we have called this mastery. He gives it poetic form and thus transcends the mundane, neurotic anxieties, that cataclysm tends to engender in us. His lifelong fascination—an obsession really—with the logic of the flow of water and how he brought it to the highest artistic expression is poetics at work.

Poetics is the revelation of meaning in life, and a meaningful life is what we are pursuing. The True Artist has the great advantage of having a way to give form to the happenings of life; it is also their special task. No matter how strange or crazy what others do seems to us, we can be sure that in their minds, that behavior is a move towards meaning. If they are True Artists, they will turn it into artistry.

It is said that in us human beings, the universe becomes aware of itself. In us, the universe is no longer just organically happening, it is now reflecting upon its own processes by means of human beings. Thomas Huxley, the 19th century thinker, biologist, and evolutionist saw three stages of evolution, the primary one being spontaneous, biological, unconscious, and instinctive; things just happened and that, for example, is how we ended up with two eyes and not one. We have two, and it is unlikely we will grow an extra one at any time. Even if we did, it would not be by conscious design. It seems that phase of evolution is settled for now. The second phase of evolution Huxley terms "technological." Here humans become able to gain control over the natural processes by means of tools, scientific discoveries, and the resulting understanding that the universe is governed by laws. That the universe can be understood at all is a major step in human evolution. Then, as part of evolution, we learn to make use of these laws.

The third phase of evolution, and this is the most momentous of all, most tenuous and fragile as well, is an expansion of consciousness. Conscious development is something we can only do for ourselves; it is not done to us or for us; we ourselves are in charge here. We are therefore an integral part of the evolution of existence. Becoming conscious cannot be done collectively, we must work this out within ourselves. From this consciousness alone comes meaning. This understanding of ourselves and our evolving was pioneered many thousands of years ago by deep thinkers in India and gathered in a body of wisdom literature that is collectively called the Upanishads. It predates Western science by many centuries but is supremely scientific in that it refuses to give credence to anything that is not verifiable. Here the verification is within the human mind itself. Modern science has been catching up with these ancient insights. There is astounding beauty in this melding of modern scientific insight and ancient wisdom.

This third phase of evolution is the True Artist's domain. They give the suggestive hints for everyone's individual search for meaning in life, it is the True Artist's allotted task in society. The iconic actor and singer Harry Belafonte once said that "artists have a valuable function in society, because it is the artists who reveal society to itself." Doctors heal the sick, lawyers help settle disputes, police make our world safe, True Artists reveal meaning. In big ways and in small ways, this is ultimately what art is all about, and why it has always been part of any society. We give it the name of poetics, the essential quality of art making, bringing to light meaning. Meaning is a fugitive little bird that will escape your grasp if you try to capture and cage it. Poetics for us then is part of the erotic dimension of life. Eroticism, though often equated solely with sexual desire, refers to the whole field of soul, of beauty, of meaning and inter-relatedness. Art for the True Artist is in the service of all these things. Poetry is elemental, not superfluous. One of poetry's most ancient compositional strategies is rhyming words. Rhyme gets our attention and establishes connection. It affects us in the way the flow of music does, depending on a repeat-pattern of sound. In fact, the word "rhyme" is directedly related to the word "rhythm." The popularity of rap music with its seeming disregard for what passes as "culture" employs yet that age-old compositional strategy. Pulsating rhythms punctuated by words that rhyme and often do not make much sense other than that they rhyme. But the fact that they rhyme magically sets up its own meaning. Such is the power of poetics. As stated before, poetry goes beyond language by means of that very same language; it gets new meaning either through rhyme or special constellations of words. This goes also for the visual language of the painter, photographer, and sculptor. It plumbs the depths of life's experiences and reveals their meaning, by means of how we ordinarily experience life.

There is a wonderful anecdote about this from one of America's foremost poet laureates, Robert Frost. After having read aloud some of his poetry, a woman from the audience asked him something to the effect of "...that last poem you read, what does it mean?" "What?" replied Frost with poetic accuracy. "Do you want me to say it again but in worse English?" In other words, he had said what he wanted to say in exactly the best way he knew how, and that was his poetry. We somehow believe that poetry can be explained, but that is exactly what it is not—an explanation of life—rather it is an expansion of life.

In the same way, dreams cannot be explained and are the deep poetic layer of our own being. Learning to listen to your dreams (which would require a whole new book) is more like listening to music, and music of a high complexity. Our dreams are the product of the alchemical workshop of our mind asleep. We cook up the most amazing meanings using the ingredients of waking life in the most astonishing and surprising constellations. They do not make sense

CHAPTER TEN

in the everyday way we make sense of things, and just like poetry using the words we use every day to go beyond their everyday meaning, dreams make sense in a deeper than rational way. They may use visual language of the outer world (though not exclusively so), but that language is put in a different order, serving a very different purpose than making sense of the visible world. They are logical, but in a non-rational way. Here again we see that things can be logical in a different way: psycho—logical; making sense in a soulful way ("psyche"–meaning "soul" or "breath" from the old Greek). Poetry transcends ordinary language, while using ordinary language, whether in words or image, and thus reveals a greater truth.

CHAPTER ELEVEN
Van Gogh as Poetic Witness

It is known that Van Gogh, the modern model of the True Artist (as Da Vinci was the model for the pre-modern age) certainly wanted to be financially successful and gain some acceptance, though he never really attained it. It must have bothered him that his brother, Theo, who was employed in one of the great art houses in Paris, was not somehow able to get him a place at the art table, or a spot on the gallery wall. How come Theo did not seem able to advocate for his struggling brother? In this curious fact, I see wrapped up some of the suggestive hints we are exploring to get at the "True" in the designation of True Artist. Over the years I have come to regard this perplexing reality of the Van Gogh brothers in a way that I have not found elsewhere, but which I believe should have been dealt with in the extensive literature dedicated to the life of Van Gogh. I cannot substantiate my view with hard facts, but I offer an understanding of human psychology and the ways of the unconscious that I think make a convincing case and throw another light on the issues of destiny we have been dealing with. Van Gogh as poetic witness was not an isolated phenomenon.

Being a painter in the fabled nineteenth century Paris, the center of the Western art world then, meant being part of or near the cultural elite. Vincent was part of that and got

CHAPTER ELEVEN

to know the famous ones, like Toulouse Lautrec. He studied with the same master Lautrec studied under for a while, and knew Pissarro, Monet, and Gauguin, with whom he lived temporarily. They all seemed dedicated to being poetic witness to their times; poetics was in the air then. However, it was also a hard struggle for recognition in that very competitive environment just as it is now.

Theo knew the art world of his day. He was one of the people in the know in Paris, an established art dealer, as the books say. Most of what we know about Vincent is by way of the letters written to Theo. It seems strange that Theo was not able to see the worth of his brother's art. After all, his brother's art would eventually sweep the world! Did he not have that extra sense that a man in his position is likely to have? Something does not make sense.

What is the psychological truth here? There seems to have been a real loving bond between the brothers, Vincent and Theo. At some point they even shared an apartment in Paris. It has always seemed to me that Vincent must have been, for Theo, part of his own essence or to some extent his counterpart. Vincent was clearly the soul of the family and younger brother Theo may have wanted to keep it that way, pure and real. Unconsciously he may have had a real reluctance to subjugate his brother's work to the vagaries of the commercial world. Perhaps he even felt that this would be detrimental to the course of Vincent's endeavors. His knowledge of the inner workings of the art world may have spurred him to spare his brother the spoilage of success, knowing intimately his delicate condition.

I have not read all the books on Van Gogh, and do not intend to do so, there are too many, but the way I just described it, is how the story always reverberated in my mind. It seems Vincent was the "tintinnayo" of his family, the name Italians give to the "family oracle," the one who is tuned into the realities of the soul and the spirit, while his brother Theo was the one turned towards the world outside, the world of business. They belonged together in a deep way, in the way Jacob and Esau of the Hebrew Bible belonged together; Jacob being the one turned inward, and Esau being the one turned outward to the world. Vincent turned his gaze on the outside world as his subject matter but used his vision to portray an inner reality. That is the very essence of poetics as we spoke of it, a poetic witnessing. It is what makes his work reverberate in so many souls all over the world. It comes from a finely tuned soulfulness. It goes deeper and wider than the ostensible subject matter. He saw right through the subject matter to the essence of it. He was a True Artist, a true poetic witness.

There is also the less attractive dimension of the story, which is also indicative of the shadow side of the poetic witness in our own time. Vincent seems to have been addicted to absinthe, a very strong drink pioneered in France by the still famous Pernod company, very fashionable until it was banned. With strong hallucinogenic properties, absinthe claimed many addicts who succumbed to its siren call. There is a beautiful drawing by Edgar Degas of Vincent sitting in a café over a glass of absinthe, a very distinctive type of glass with a spoon laid on top. Absinthe is another aspect of the Van Gogh story which is not much talked about, though it explains a lot. It was called "the green muse" because it made those "high" on it feel a definite attraction to the color green, and also produced ringing in the ears. It landed a lot of its users in mental hospitals, which is the only way they knew how to deal with those addicted then. All elements of the Van Gogh story—his paintings' famed "apple green," the trouble with his ear, no doubt a constant ringing that

CHAPTER ELEVEN

he may have meant to cut out by literally cutting off his ear, his stay in the mental hospital; all seemed connected to his affinity for absinthe. Additionally, there is the story that he presented his cut-off ear to a prostitute, inspired by seeing a bullfight in the famous Roman arena in Arles, where after the killing of the bull, the toreador would cut off one of the bull's ears to give to a favored lady in the audience. It seems Vincent may have somehow re-enacted that scenario. It is a horrifying story really, and speaks of a severe mental disturbance, a consequence of drugs.

The fact that Degas, already famous, knew Vincent and took time to draw him sitting some distance from him in a café is the other dimension of the Van Gogh story often overlooked in favor of the "suffering for his art" dimension, more favored in the popular mind. He was recognized as part of that intensely creative climate in Paris of the late 19th and early 20th century. He was as much a part of "the scene" as Basquiat was part of the New York scene, grasped out of obscurity by Andy Warhol. He was certainly not a lonely shooting star in the way people like to portray him; he was part of what is still considered a special time in world art history. Today, we are isolated, despite the virtual community online.

Theo and Vincent remained connected in a deep way and theirs was a collective fate. Theo died not long after Vincent took his own life and while Theo had a family, a wife and child to live for, his demise does not seem like happenstance, but rather seems to point to a deeper alliance.

It is not too far-fetched to identify the True Artist as the "tintinnayo" of society. They are the poetic witness, a low-key oracle-type person in whatever circles they move. We are always looking for "the next great thing" to come out of the art world, the new avant-garde, the latest something or other, but it may not come in the way that we are accustomed to look for it. Society's True Artists are "a-stray and lost in the villages," as Ezra Pound says in his poem, "The Rest." They cater often to their immediate circle and are important there as builders of culture, and keepers of the flame of culture.

The Van Gogh story then touches on many of the characteristic elements of the True Artist's life. But it does so in an exaggerated way and as such can be misleading for many on the road. In that way, indeed, as mentioned before, Van Gogh's shadow hangs over every art exhibit and somehow puts every art display in perspective. It also hangs as a shadow over the lives of many True Artists struggling to find their destiny. His work is truly great and stands on its own, but the preoccupation with his suffering is misplaced. Tragedy enhances greatness in the popular imagination, but in reality it may be more of a morbid fascination.

CHAPTER TWELVE
Mastery

Mastery demands all of the person.
—Albert Einstein

Ultimately all poetics rest on a foundation of practical know-how; there is no substitute for technical proficiency. Technical proficiency is the foundation of mastery. Poetics is artistic intelligence embedded in proficiency. Mastery is technical know-how meeting up with imagination flowing from the depths of the True Artist's sense of destiny. Mastery is artistic intelligence supported by solid know-how. Artistic intelligence is the poetic dimension. It is an ability to look deeply into all aspects of life, and the ability to give it form, led by that insight. Some will call this the philosophical side of things. In the original sense of the word philosophy is love (philo) of wisdom (sophia). It is not a penchant for thinking, it is a *love* of wisdom. And "love" is the erotic dimension of life, erotic in the widest sense of the word, as a flower is erotic in how it attracts bees or dazzles our eyes with its beauty. Artistic intelligence includes having a sense of where you feel you belong in the long march of human creativity through the ages. Artistic intelligence (the other A.I.!) is also what gives us a sense of who we are amid the powerful technological innovations that are coming at us with amazing speed, impacting us both positively and negatively.

On the proscenium above the stage at Royce Hall, a major performance hall at the University of California at Los Angeles it says: "Education is learning to use the tools that the succeeding generations have found to be indispensable." Yet we live in an era in which much of whatever happened before we came on the scene is dismissed, or severely challenged. History is full of our friends though; people like us who were struggling to make sense of their life and times and came up with things we can benefit from and employ in creating what has meaning for others. Of course, it is right that we should question what went before, sifting the issues, seeing how certain things remain while others go by the wayside. Our artistic intelligence is molded by our questioning and learning. "Never stop questioning," Albert Einstein said. There have been and still are religious traditions that consider questioning sinful and a kick against "the faith." Yet all kids are born questioners. The True Artist is one who never grows out of that. They just grow up into questioners with growing insight and the wherewithal to give form to what they know. Our most profound questions are not answered by science, they are answered in the realm of poetics.

In this questioning, mastery is of the essence for the True Artist, an inescapable part. Without it, whatever vision we have, whatever insights we may want to offer, do not amount to much. Mastery is the carrier wave of all we do. So, here we finally find something that we feel we can depend on. There is no True Artist without the pursuit of mastery. I will show a little later how this is already intuitively understood especially by young people, though how to approach it, is not. What are some of the steps that must be taken to achieve mastery? What has proven effective? We first must understand what mastery really is. Mastery is not mysterious, but it needs to be rightly understood. Saying that someone has "mastered" a certain subject, an instrument, a computer program, is from our viewpoint, an incorrect use of the word. With it, we are merely saying that someone has gained technical proficiency; has acquired a skill. While that is part of mastery, it is not mastery yet. Being skillful has a lot of power and joy in it but is only a first—and necessary—step on the road to mastery. There is no mastery without superior technical ability. Yet there can be superior technical ability without mastery. It is good to know the difference. Expertise is relatively easy to get. It can be learned in many places; nowadays online we may garner great skills. It is never easy, but because expertise is the thing that can be most easily organized and taught, there are lots of opportunities to get it; many venues are open. Since it always requires commitment and discipline, the best way to start gathering expertise is by concentrating on something that you are naturally attracted to; that will give you the staying power necessary in the long process of gathering. It is important to ask yourself, "What do I want to become an expert in?" Your immediate answer will be quite clear, even if it may not pass the test of what is most practical. It is often said that expertise in one area translates into expertise in other areas. Although this is true, it is still best to start with something that you feel a natural inclination towards. We will discuss this later when discussing drawing. If you are not sure, just write down some of your choices and it will soon be clear enough. Or you can use the method advocated by none other than Benjamin Franklin. Write down what you feel attracted to and then make two columns, a pro and a con column. Start writing down the arguments—pro in one column, the arguments against in the other—then look at which list is longer. It may make the decision a bit easier to reach once you realize that becoming an expert in something is not a final destination, but merely a first part of the journey. No matter how essential, expertise is but a first steppingstone on our way to mastery. Again, we must not confuse "mastering" a technique or skill with being a master. Even the dictionary definition of mastery as "gaining control of something" is off the mark for us. Skill is a part of mastery, but mastery is wide, expertise narrow. In ancient Egypt and in other societies as well, its artists, its craftspeople, were considered part of the "magician class." In that bit of knowledge, we can glimpse some of the meaning of mastery, which is more than just command of a certain skill set. The word magician has as one of its root words "mag" which means "more" and can also be found in words like magnet, magnification, magnificent. In the manner of the magician, gaining mastery is "becoming larger." Some attribute the origin of the word "mag" to an ancient Greek island where magnetic ore was discovered: Maga. And let us not forget that the compass works on magnetic impulses as well, ever pointing to one point on earth: North. In like manner, mastery also points toward a stable point: our north, our home, our destiny. Like a magnet attracting iron filings, mastery is a "becoming larger." It is a skill set that attracts to itself, like a magnet, those elements which make it expand beyond itself. Mastery is where expertise—through continual practice—becomes infused with wider knowledge, opening the door for intuition to come in, and express itself as poetics.

Mastery then can be seen as infusing a well-honed skill set with our personality. While many opportunities are open to us for acquiring skills, established art schools and university art departments seem to be abandoning basic skill sets for ideologies about making art. But aspiring young artists know better. Many students, often from well-known universities or institutions of art both in the US and abroad, came to our college, known for its emphasis on skill development, because they had the distinct sense that they had not been well served. "I didn't learn anything," was a phrase I heard from many. Without a solid base to stand on there is no way, I repeat, *no way* to assess the things you are being taught. How can you possibly know whether what you are learning is right for you if you cannot perform your art. We must gain good skill sets because that is what gives us the freedom to determine our own path. Skills, being rather straight forward, are relatively easy to acquire. There are many great instruction books from long ago and from right now, along with thousands of online materials, which can give you much what you need for skill development. I believe that skill is best developed in a face-to-face classroom or working studio sitting with people interacting and a teacher present. On your own it is easy to get lost. Classes are also good because few of us have the self-discipline or the guiding instinct to search out what we need to know. A teacher can direct you as to when and what to address more easily. They also hold you accountable, and most of us need that.

    I have lots of books of art instruction and philosophy of art, and often it is just one or two ideas in them that strike me and that justify the purchasing price. From some I get nothing more than a lead into a next phase of inquiry. Sometimes the best information I obtain from a book is on the first random page I happen to open the book on when I first get it. It is a bit of a haphazard method and does not work for everyone, for sure. Going through the table of contents and seeing what attracts my eye and what seems to interest me is another important way to approach it. When I come across things that I find compelling in a book, I start my own private index on the blank pages in the back of the book by noting a page number along with the subject matter, thereby creating my own reference tool. For example, I may have a back-of-the-book inscription that says "p.72: virtuosity in art" and then I may expand on that later if I find the same subject on a different page, I simply add "p.116/p.72: Virtuosity in art." Over the years patterns of interest begin to arise, and I can go through the indices rather quickly searching for a topic, which is great when I need something for my own work, a lecture, or a workshop. If you like to read on a Kindle or other digital device, you can create your own lists of notes there as well. I take it with me when I travel, since one small device can hold a whole library, together with my own notes and underlining (even on my smart phone). This is mind blowing to me, since I was accustomed to carrying around heavy books in bags on airplanes and in cars. I spent a lot of time in libraries, and I do miss the atmosphere of concentration found there, but now you can access any information on a laptop. The ease with which we access so many ideas has, alas, also made these things seem less significant. Somehow their easy availability has diminished their importance. Having to search through a library catalogue, going through the stacks to find it, somehow deepens your interest and connection in whatever you are searching for. A bonus too, are the books you happen to come across while searching for what you want.

    This is all part of the fabric of mastery in that it allows you to make your own decisions of what is important to you and what is not. The easy access to information of all types, in a strange and roundabout way, has strengthened the position of the True Artist. Since nearly all information has become readily accessible and available to all, it seems that it would be hard to establish your own individuality amidst it all. Yet, there is something that is not accessible to all. There is something that escapes the conceitful grasp of A.I. creators—the poetic dimension. And through this, the True Artist, almost exclusively, escapes the ravenous scrutiny of A.I. with its reductionistic claws of technology and its guiding ideology. The True Artist can stand proudly and untouched amid the spectacle and creative carnage brought about by technology. They will try to convince you that A.I. makes learning a skill and achieving mastery obsolete, but it is just the opposite. The pseudo prophets of technology are great technicians, but few are masters of anything.

We wrongfully believe that our times are not capable of producing greatness. It is true that greatness, the best the human spirit is capable of, must be supported by a societal climate of accomplishment and a desire for excellence. It is the True Artist's work and being that affects the collective consciousness of a people. To the politically minded that observation seems out of touch, impractical, and foolish, but True Artists know that it is exactly the very essence of their work. It is culture building and that demands the kind of heroic spirit that often seems tapped out in prosperous societies. It is the willingness of a true radical to stand aside and observe and know what is needed because of what he or she has found within him—or herself. Driven by an inner awareness, cultivated on the path, and as always, backed up by mastery, he or she intuits what is needed on the level of our being human. The word "radical" comes from the Latin word "radix" meaning roots, and thus what is "radical" in its essence refers to something fundamental in society, a quintessential something inherent in the collective. This may be why in contemporary slang, when people say "wow, that is radical," they mean that it is great and wonderful! "Radical, man!" says one student seeing the work of another. It is mostly used to indicate a fanatical, revolutionary stance, a societal militancy. This is almost exactly the opposite of what honors the essential nature, the roots of society. A quote often attributed to Gandhi, but most likely said in 1918 by a trade union activist in New York of all people, says, "First they ignore you. Then they ridicule you. And then they attack you and want to burn you. And then they build monuments to you." The true radical, in the original sense of the word "radical," works on the essence of our togetherness, while someone with a militant disposition, whom we more commonly call "a radical," seeks to destroy it.

It is the True Artist's mission to build that togetherness, but not as an ideologue of some sort, but as someone through whom the wisdom of the age flows and comes out as work. A well—rooted culture makes a healthy society and advances human evolution. There is a need for struggle which, in a society accustomed to comfort, we are not inclined to engage in. The need to struggle is however an essential part of our being human, often called the warrior instinct. If it has become dormant, that does not mean it has disappeared; being an essential part of us it will exert itself one way or the other. Without artful mastery it goes into political strife, however this does not touch culture, but hides it. There is then a definite sense of struggle for a True Artist. He or she is used to it from the get-go; the battle to be true to one's destiny prepares one for such battles. No matter the outward success, it remains a humble life, because coming face-to-face with the seemingly intractable problems of human society and the unchanging character of human nature (the one constant at all times!), means coming in touch with it within oneself, and that cannot but humble you. Any outward display of grandiose solutions is by its very nature immediately suspect to the True Artist. Human nature being unchanging, it will always be so. During the fabled Renaissance, when culture was "high" culture and appreciated even by people lower on the societal ladder, brutality was never far off, and powerful and cruel leaders like Cesar Borgia, or marauding armies from England or France were ever present. During the same time as the Renaissance in Europe, in the rest of the world the slaughter and oppression of people by power-seeking elites is shocking to read. To be a culture builder—a keeper of the flame—is not a call to arms, but a call to strive for the best humans are capable of; more precisely, a call to pursue that which only humans are uniquely capable of: deep insight, deep intuition, complex emotional response. Machines may be capable of reasoning to a certain extent, but they are incapable of impassioned insight into human life. They have no body; they do not exist. There is no inner fire in machines, no eros, no love, no poetry. Love is non-rational, though not ir-rational. There is a French saying: "The heart has its reasons that reason does not understand." This could be adjusted to say that the heart has its reasons that a computer cannot understand, when love is made visible, in its light as well as in its darker aspects. The True Artist is the unseen builder, the way the great craftsmen and architects who built the great medieval cathedrals were. They made decorations that were invisible to the eye of one looking up at the magnificent structures. They were the gift of the artist to his task. The cathedral builders were devout in their dedication and were often from families that had given several generations to the project, as it often took a hundred years or more to finish the task. Even in the gargoyles, that you see on so many old churches and cathedrals, often cleverly hidden, fantastical beasts, dragons, evil looking creatures all, and not at all Christian symbols, you see the builders giving dimension to the religious experience. Armed with modern psychological insights, especially those of depth psychology, we can see in them interesting symbols and reminders of the darker aspects of existence, even in places dedicated to divine light! The True Artist looks at all aspects of life, and not just one side of it.

CHAPTER THIRTEEN
The Yoda Principle

THE NATURAL INSTINCT FOR MASTERY

Many young people instinctively know that mastery is something to be desired. Of course, mastery in itself is exciting and gives a sense of self-worth like nothing else can and therefore makes life more meaningful. Young people have not had their dreams and enthusiasms "cut down to size" yet, and so mastery, along with many other things, is naturally seen as desirable. Many young people, and those already grown, show their enthusiasm by the way they devour graphic novels, comics, movies, and videogames about a "master" of some sort (usually martial arts), becoming teacher to a worthy but "unwashed" pupil, giving him or her the strength that comes from mastery, thereby empowering the pupil's life. Some call it the "Yoda principle," borrowing the name from the impish wise master character from the Star Wars movies.

Often the "student" is picked out by the master because the pupil is not aware of their own inherent power. The master sees through the youthful folly and teaches discipline to channel and bring out the slumbering power. The master can see the potential and knows what the pupil needs. Even in simple animation stories there is that extra psycho-spiritual dimension which is that necessary component for turning expertise into mastery. Native American tribes, often known for being great warriors, valued the innate warrior spirit of their young men as a gift from the gods to the tribe, needed for its survival and protection. The shaman or medicine person of the tribe would also pick out those who exactly should not be warriors but rather part of their special circle of shamanic discipline and mastery. Both were honored and harnessed for their proper purposes.

Young people instinctively feel that contemporary society, with its modernist conceits, has no place for either their warrior spirit or spiritual energy just spoken of, and denigrates them. That way it deprives them of something that they intuitively value and feel deep within themselves. Society is thereby deprived of some of its greatest potential, and many born to fulfill those tasks are left confounded and stranded on the fringes of society. More than that, without proper channeling, those great natural gifts tend to turn inside out and run rampant, because they do not die off or somehow magically disappear. What is meant for being creative and constructive, for example, will come out in destructive ways, either self-destructive or destructive to society. Better to honor them and give them proper master training.

The current enthusiasm for martial arts may be one expression of an organic longing for mastery. Young people somehow know that they have something that is precious that needs to be properly cultivated. If it is not given a place, the young person mourns it as a sad loss in life. The desire for mastery training is the natural antidote. Mastery gives us a platform from which to survey our world, the rest of our life, and the situation at hand. Competitive young athletes often have a sense of confidence and assuredness that most

CHAPTER THIRTEEN

of his fellows lack. He or she is good at something and has a discipline which directs and adds power to their lives.

People going to martial arts studios, or yoga studios, or art and drawing classes, are displaying what I call that instinct for mastery. Those with the True Artist destiny do not have an academy for True Artists to attend, but they gain expertise, the corner stone of mastery, in many places. A friend of mine likes to say that the only True Artist Academy exists only in a galaxy far, far away. The True Artist must find the elements of his or her mastery here and now and piece it all together. It is The Great Work described in the vernacular of the secret brotherhoods which we will mention later. We embark on this pursuit of mastery, not out of desire, but from inner necessity. The real challenge, and the real subject of this book, is finding our ways through all the different experiences and expertise that pull us in so many different directions and come out with a more focused sense of our destiny. Gaining expertise in something close to our destiny's trajectory is not only an important pillar of our destiny, but also a formidable starting point.

The True Artist is different from those who pursue expertise for expertise's sake or for virtuosity's sake. True Artists know the joy and satisfaction that comes from virtuosic competence, but also know that it may obscure our true destiny trajectory. Once you get good at drawing, for example, really find your ease with it, you feel loathe to go beyond it and become a beginner again in a wider or different area of challenge. George Leonard in his book *Mastery* says that to become a master, you must be willing to be a fool again. That becomes more and more difficult the more sophisticated you have become. It is said that the master's mind and the beginner's mind are one and the same in the end. In fact, we become masters exactly because we want to give powerful expression to all that grabbed us about life before we got all cultured and knowledgeable. Mastery for the artist is knowing how to manage those unruly, instinctive energies that arise from deep within and would overtake us if we did not have a solid skillset in place. The True Artist master is in touch with those energies in him—or herself because those are the things he or she wants to give proper form to. If we get stuck in the so-called "pride of proficiency," we experience the fate that the French writer Honoré Balzac, in his wonderful small booklet *The Unknown Masterpiece,* speaks of regarding a beautiful young woman. He writes about how such a young woman loses some of her special attractiveness when she learns to manage her self-presentation to the world. The special attractiveness she had was the spontaneous emergence of who she was. Mastery for the True Artist is being in touch with the poetics of the unintended and using it in his or her work without diminishing or "civilizing" it.

As I was writing this a young deer came by my writing window and looked at me with that wonder that I used to have as a kid. We stared at each other, and I was careful not to make a sudden move which would scare it away. It is like that with kids, you can scare them away from their natural and beautiful wonder about everything. We can scare off our innate sensitivity and openness to life by all too sudden movements of life. Just as the young fawn comes equipped for the life he is to live, so does the True Artist, though he or she may doubt it for many years! The work that awaits is to make all the gifts and talents that we already possess come to fruition. The True Artist must learn to give form to what lies within. Deer do not have to bother with that because they are fully equipped for the natural environment they live in (upgraded by the beautiful tulips we planted, and which

CHAPTER THIRTEEN

are apparently wonderful to eat!). The natural habitat of the True Artist is life itself and the True Artist is at home in the confusing multitude of its expressions. There is nothing in life that is not part of our trajectory, nothing we merely visit, all is education, experience, and edification which, if it is backed by mastery, results in our life's art.

I integrated this way of looking at things in teaching composition for many years. Having to study the matter more deeply—which is one wonderful aspect of being a teacher—I came to the formulation that "nothing is not part of the composition." By this is meant that once you have your visual field (paper, canvas, panel, screen) and start to make marks on it, your composition has started and everything you do or do not do within that field is part of the composition. Even those parts which have "nothing" done to them are part of it. There is nothing that is *not* part of the composition. Even those parts that you have left "open" or unresolved (and leaving some parts unattended may be just what is needed), are a definite part of the composition. Understanding that was a great advance in my own work—and in life. Even those things you have left unattended or avoided doing are still part of the overall composition of your life. I look for those "unfinished" parts of great artists' works and wonder why they left it as such; the true master does not leave things unattended without intent.

Something that I find comforting about great master pieces of art is that you can always trust them. You can look at them and ask the work: why is that thing here, and not there? Why did you not do this or that, start this and not finish that? You can ask those questions because you know that the master has a master's eye and has been there and called it "good" the way it is. Besides living teachers helping us to attain mastery, we have those silent masters who are still here through the work they left behind, hanging on museum walls or accessible on a website. It is not so much about picking up technical tips from them but seeing or thinking the way they did. "Do not follow the masters, seek what they sought," I was once taught. While we now get things mainly from the computer screen (and hopefully from some good art books), there were times when artists were able to set up an easel in the museum and copy work directly. I was fortunate to have been able to do that when I was a museum art guard in the local Norton Simon Museum in Pasadena, California. On the days it was closed I was allowed to set up an easel in the galleries and copy directly from the works of some great masters there. I can confidently say that there is no substitute. You penetrate the very fabric of a work when you copy it directly. At some point, a certain confluence starts to happen, and you feel truly in tune with the master whom you are copying. It was not so much my intention to copy the work as to penetrate the spirit of it. I wanted to feel what had gone into making it. It is a most amazing type of experience. Mister Norton Simon himself, would come by and share in the experience with me! He loved his museum and took a hands-on interest in it.

A great artist like Paul Cézanne, who is known for his innovative ways, would do exactly that. He would set up an easel in no less a place than the Louvre in Paris, to copy the masters directly; alas you can no longer do that. Cézanne claimed that he wanted to paint as if no one had ever painted before. This seems to be in contradiction to his weekly visits to the Louvre to copy the masters. It seems contradictory but it is not, because he was not copying so much as entering the spirit of a work. That is indeed what happens when you "copy" directly—you are made to participate in a search for meaning. It is an experience that recalibrates your inner

CHAPTER THIRTEEN

settings. But even making a copy from a website image can give much of that experience, though it cannot replace a direct contact.

Being an art guard in the museum was one of those significant episodes in my life, and a worthwhile mental attic memory.[1] I felt happy doing it. The job became one of absorbing great works of art by being in their continual presence. My soul felt quite at home in the museum environment. I must be honest and remind myself that while I was barely on the path, the fledgling True Artist part of me, was saying to the masters that surrounded me all day long, quietly and bashfully: "I am one of you guys!" I would not have dared speak that truth out loud, not even to myself, because I would have thought it absurd or even crazy, but deep inside that is how it was. I understood them on a deep level, even if I could not hold a candle to them and had not achieved anything worth writing home about.

Of course, when I would come home at night, tired of standing all day (we were not allowed to sit down), I did not quite feel so much one with the masters I had to guard, for I was still working on gaining proficiency.

---

1   I made a painting with the title "ArtGuard2000;" which celebrated some of that experience; it was part of exhibitions traveling from Harvard University to museums in Italy, Florence and Palermo.

CHAPTER FOURTEEN
A Secret Brotherhood

Most of us of the True Artist temperament have a positive and natural desire for a mentor. We have a deep instinctive feel for how things would be best handled and the complexities of the path before us. We intuit the wholeness of the enterprise in moments of clarity, moments which often quickly dissipate and dissolve into the everydayness of our lives. Those moments of clarity remembered are enough to carry us a long way, but the forgetting may become semi-permanent. We may have memory flashbacks of what once stood so clearly before our eyes then often dismiss them as "childhood flights of fancy" or "pipe dreams." All these are common themes of the True Artist path.

The desire for a mentor or guide in our own times is usually fulfilled in phases and installments. The urgency of the desire for a mentor may lead us to bestow the aura of mentorship on some who are not worthy of it. These difficult experiences become lessons to learn from. They are disappointments that may even feel like betrayal but ultimately, they feel that way because of our own too fervent desires. The times we live in are not suited for an ongoing relationship of that sort. However, you learn to take your mentorship in small doses, which you then must cobble together into a coherent whole. In fact, it has never been different in history. Even when those kinds of master-student apprentice relationships were prevalent, for the True Artist there would inevitably come a time when it became essential to break with the master. This is a natural part of the path of the True Artist as well. You may read about this in many biographies of great artists of such a period. Eventually a break would come, and had to come, because the True Artist needs to be independent. It is in the nature of things like mentorship that some disappointment will follow when you come to see that your mentor is just a human being with flaws and shortcomings. We start to find fault with those we have put our trust in when we come face-to-face with the fact that it was our own need for a person on a pedestal that made us seek mentorship. However, we should never dismiss the importance of mentorships-by-installment!

Modern society seems to promote an overall psychic instability, which is the price we pay for social and physical mobility. We are forced to find the needed stability within ourselves and in the way we approach our work. This being "condemned to freedom," as existential philosophers call it, is exactly the terrain for the True Artist to work in. The True Artist is always busy in tending those fields of psychological welfare, whether it is in minor or major ways. Conscious of their positions in society, True Artists work on the deeper levels of stability of the human psyche.

I had three major mentors, or people whom I would designate as such. There were also minor mentors—people who had a definite impact on my life, big or small, and who were more than friendly advisers. There were others whom I remember fondly because they took a kindly interest in me. Not all were in the art field and that inner multiplicity is part of the peculiar nature of my path. They all become united in the core of the *True Artist Destiny*. One of the great defining aspects of a true mentorship relationship is that it is more than just expertise, knowledge, or wisdom being passed on. There is such a thing as "transmission," which is the very essence of it. It is not definable other than that mentor and mentee each have a definite sense of it. It is a near magical process of being "initiated" in being an artist. You are no longer a struggling soul; you are now an artist on the path, in line with the processes practiced for centuries.

One of my main art mentors hinted in no unsubstantial ways that there was and always had been such a process, part of some kind of secret brotherhood (sisters included no doubt), who saw themselves as the guardians of the essential character of the True Artist. That brotherhood could not be found in some directory (not even in a search engine), and that was part of its power. Belonging to it was not a matter of signing up or registering like you would for art school but was accomplished through a complicated process of invitation and being vetted. You may not have even been aware that this was happening, that you were being considered as a potential "initiate." This supposed brotherhood, like other secret brotherhoods in history, existed in all different cultures in some form or another. It existed to safeguard noble purposes and secrets, which in the hands of the unqualified would become corrupted. This can be seen throughout history and certainly nowadays. The progress of technology has made the advances in art, science, and philosophy, readily available to anyone, which leads to them becoming disfigured in the hands of those ignorant of its deeper purposes.

Though I have never been keen on speculating on unseen and hidden forces in what is going on in the world, this all connected with things I had been thinking, feeling, and wishing for. My interest was in something dedicated to higher and nobler purposes, out of reach of the corrupting influences of established institutions. I think about the

CHAPTER FOURTEEN

themes in anime, popular animation, and video games my students were hooked on. There the story line is often about secret societies dedicated to fighting the good fight, erasing evil from this earth, and establishing the good. This theme runs through many stories of superheroes as well. These stories satisfy some hunger in young (and old) souls.

My mentor talked about this (these secret brotherhoods) while doing other things and as if not really wanting to make a big deal of it. At the same time, he apparently wanted me to know about it. I never dared to ask him outright whether he himself was connected with any such brotherhood or was himself one of the "initiates." I just never could muster the courage to do so outright. Had I been able to do so, it would probably have made no difference.

Whenever I would press him on these issues, he would get irritated with me, as if I was making it all up, and I could never bring myself to remind him that it was he who had brought up these issues. Annoyed, he would only tell me to get on with the work. I learned to not bring up the subject, although I wanted to; I wanted to know all about it. He would sometimes lapse into some kind of reverie and say things which sounded to me like he was "in the know." This was like lifting the veil just a bit. I let him go on at those times and knew most of all not to interrupt him, ask questions, or let slip even a slight eagerness to know more. I became good at feigning disinterest, while being intensely interested. I knew that if I brought up the subject at all, no matter how obliquely, he would deflect as if I had dreamed up the whole thing. He would make me feel ridiculous, as if I was way too excited about such a thing. Still, the whole enterprise of being part of such a secret brotherhood (which I assumed was for artists) filled me with excitement. A gathering of artists with high aspirations was what I always felt was lacking in the art world I had come to know. I have been in wonderful and on-going get-togethers of truly serious and amazing artists, but the dimension of a ritualized initiation with definite standards was missing of course. I never mentioned this kind of thing to any of them and now feel I should have. I am sure that they would have related in some way.

At one point, an old friend of my mentor's came to visit. This friend had apparently done a lot for my mentor and was welcomed in their home. My mentor's wife was not too keen on him because he behaved quite like a higher-up and expected to be served as such. Being a modern woman, independent and accomplished as an artist in her own right, this was not something she took kindly to. She was a woman of considerable spiritual insight and may have been in on whatever her husband supposedly was part of, but she never touched the subject. If I would bring it up, feigning only a passing interest, she would kind of shrug it off as if to say that she found this all to be something typical of her husband; apparently, she did not put much stock in it.

Still the way they treated their visitor, and the way certain topics seemed to go unspoken, never mentioned, made me wonder. I felt to be part of a certain atmosphere of influence, though I would not have been able to put words to it, not then, not now. Of course, once you have begun to speculate, any innocent occurrences get scrutinized for some deeper meaning which they may or may not have.

My mentor's many tantalizing hints that he knew of some kind of brotherhood and may even have belonged to one are still with me, but this did not make me go on a dramatic search for hidden dimensions of the artist's life. However, I learned from this that I am invested, emotionally as well as intellectually, in some standards that transcend the mudslinging fest of opposing opinions that characterize a modern society, and its art world dimension. I also understood the impulse to protect them from being devalued and demeaned. I found that the near-religious belief in progress, which has become an unexamined maxim of the modern mind, was not mine. The very subject of a dedicated brotherhood inspired me, and I still have not, and do not want to, let go of the possibility of such a society existing. If there is no such society, there ought to be one! A society dedicated to the highest standards of excellence, not just of craft but also of philosophical depth and spiritual insight, seems a natural component of the True Artist destiny, and a missing dimension of modern life.

In times of great societal upheaval (as we are experiencing now) these kinds of hidden groupings would be the way to ensure continuance of the best in us until more congenial times arrive when the dormant seeds, kept safe in obscurity, can come to fruition.

THE INNER GAME OF ART

According to scholars there was and still is to some extent, a definite difference between how things of importance are taught, teacher to student, in the East and the West. In the West the pursuit of knowledge has been open and public, for all to see. In the East, certain knowledge always was considered too powerful, too fine, for greedy, jumpy minds, and in danger of being diminished that way. Therefore, the interaction between teacher and student would remain strictly confidential. Of course, much of this has changed as more and more of what was once hidden has gotten out into the open, yet the original intent of the East seems appropriate. The game of art is open to all now, but the inner game of art is not, and cannot be. With all the intrusive technologies surrounding us, there remains that inner sanctum, the habitat of the True Artist, which cannot be reached by external means. In this context it makes sense that artists at certain points of history would be regarded as part of the magicians' class.

I am not quite done with this subject for there are elements in it that shine a light on an important aspect of the True Artist life. The initiates of secret brotherhoods of which we have some knowledge, worked among the common folks, unknown to these as initiates. This hidden nature of the True Artist in society, brings up the unavoidable loneliness which is part of any True Artist path. What we know of these secret brotherhoods, apparently the highest in rank, both the initiates and their pupils, were indistinguishable from common crafts people and scholars. Some would embrace the life of an artistic professional, and as such make a living and remain on the path of the True Artist, but they are not one and the same. To the True Artist, art meant a spiritual force in society, not just a profession nor a pastime nor an amusement or diversion. And it remains so to this day. I can point to Rembrandt, a favorite of mine and many, for whom art was never just a profession, but always a spiritual pursuit. That, in True Artist's fashion, intertwined with intensely worldly interests. There is then nothing that is not part of the True Artist life.

The whole "secret brotherhood" episode with my mentor, I believe, was to teach me that you do not need a secret brotherhood, no special society, secret or not, to adhere to higher principles. The idea that something like that might exist is enough to spur us on to aspire to the highest. This has always been the underlying "secret code" of great artists. My intense desire as a young man to be recognized by someone who understood, an initiate, who could show me a better way to be what I had been all along, and guide me right, is more a part of young souls than we expect.

The Renaissance had that aspect of a brotherhood of excellence as well, and though it was deeply rooted in the Catholicism of its birthplace, it also partook of the Greek ideas that came in through the manuscripts spirited out of Constantinople (Istanbul). One of the great manuscripts we already mentioned was the *Corpus Hermeticum,* which contained some of the mystical strains that we see in the works of greats like Da Vinci, Michelangelo, Raphael, and Bernini. These are definitely not part of Catholic orthodoxy, yet they have become accepted parts of the great tradition and are celebrated as treasures of the Vatican Museum and many museums around the world. For those in the know, it is obvious. For the common viewer, the works are accessible on other levels. Again, the great essence, though in full view, goes hidden.

The intellectual atmosphere of the Renaissance came out of that text and the other books that Lorenzo de Medici had translated as soon as they came to him. Ficino, already mentioned, founded the "Platonic Academy" in Florence, which became the great magnet for scholars and artists of the day, a fountainhead of intellectual and artistic activity. From this, came the inspiration for what would become known as "the Renaissance." The deep insights that flowed from it were lost on the workers and peasant class but not on the great universal minds, the architects, painters, sculptors of the age. The ideas impregnated their works. These can be compared with the mysteries of which Pythagoras spoke and which he prohibited his students from discussing, so as not to profane them. Pythagoras (570-490 BC) was the early Greek philosopher who was the inspiration of

Socrates, Plato, and Aristotle, and thus of Western civilization in general.

"How can the ones inheriting such a grand tradition become so willfully ignorant?" a dear and learned old friend of mine once exclaimed when visiting Florence, thinking about the contemporary artist class. It is true. How can we so nonchalantly handle our inheritance as we seem to be doing? A certain madness sets in when our minds are untethered from the great minds who engineered the necessary foundations of the civilization of which we are the products.

Adapting some wisdom from Confucius, we can say that True Artists understand something deeply and report on it, while others know what sells. A creator who understands something deeply but has no craft, no language to report on it, no mastery, is not a True Artist, but is someone engaged in fanciful imaginings. Those who have craft and technique alone, are not True Artists either. They are technicians. And though they can produce amazing work, they are not True Artists. This fact makes it impossible to create a manual for success.

Johannes Vermeer, the 17th century Dutch master, who by now has become a super star world artist, was not always the world art star he is today. He was my favorite from a very young age, becoming that when I was led by my mother's hand through the museum. However, with all his now highly praised mastery, he too was hidden in plain sight for a long time. He had to be "rediscovered." His subject matter was no different from that used by many others during that same time, nor is it of itself a particularly exciting or brilliant subject matter. They are domestic scenes of no great import—a woman reading a letter by an open window or a music lesson at the keyboard of the day, the harpsichord. But, unlike the works of others of similar subjects, his work

CHAPTER FOURTEEN

connects us with life on a deeper level; it speaks of existence, not just of life in one specific period of history only, but of all time. Many of his works have a depth of rendition which reveals an understanding that goes into it and transcends the subject. The commonality of subject matter however made the cognoscenti lump Vermeer in with the lesser work of another master of that period. Vermeer literally had to be "rescued" from remaining hidden in plain sight and be reinstated. Two 19th century art experts, Waagen and Thoré-Bürger, understood and exposed the terrible injustice. While different times value different subject matter, this is not the issue—depth of insight is.

I remember being at the first (almost) comprehensive exhibit of Vermeer's work (several have followed since) at a very special museum in my hometown, The Hague, in the Netherlands. Once a royal palace, it has several great works by Vermeer, among them the now ultra-famous "Girl with the Pearl Earring," and his only landscape "View of Delft," which I have always thought to be one of the great works of art in the world. This museum is a wonderful place to visit because it seems the works truly belong there. For this exhibit they had gathered his artwork from all over the world which is no small feat. Even though it was once a royal residence, the museum has relatively small exhibition spaces and so, for this exhibit they not only had tickets for specific hours of the day, but also urged the crowds to move along. Of course, no lover of art likes that; they like to take their time with great works. As we were being moved along, I was standing next to a mother with her young boy who must have been no more than eight or ten years old. He stood transfixed looking at one of the smaller works. He would not be moved. His mother urged him to do so because the guards were trying to make place for many more still to come. He refused. He stood transfixed as if completely taken up in this small work. Now, *that* is concentration I thought! I also remember thinking that if I could ever capture the imagination of a kid like that, then I would have done something right in life and my work as an artist would not have been in vain. The True Artist works from the perspective of his or her inner kid, which is always full of wonder, always curious, always excited about something in the world. I read that the great 18th century German philosopher Emmanuel Kant who, as far as I knew did not exactly cut an exciting figure in real life and whose work can be quite dense and ponderous, was said to be like a kid in his approach to his interests. An ultra-disciplined man of strict habits whose best-known work is called "Critique of Pure Reason," his inner child remained alive and well and his great adult work came out of that spirit, which may account for his enduring legacy.

Vermeer's work exudes a deep devotional interest in the meaning of life through our experience of the visual. I am convinced that the boy at his mother's hand, mesmerized by that small work, felt it. It was, I think, also what touched me when I first stood in front of his work. It is not a scene like in other artists of that time; it is vision made *into* a scene. I have also often wondered if any of Vermeer's offspring—he had fifteen kids—ever had that kind of connection with their father's work. I doubt it. Conversely, he did not seem that interested in kids, since he never painted any of his own brood. Except for two barely defined figures in his painting of a street in his hometown Delft, he never painted children.

So, I do credit my mother for taking me to the museum like this mother standing next to me had done for her son, for it sparked in me a deep long-lasting and rather natural affection for such great work. The artists of the golden age

CHAPTER FOURTEEN

of painting in the Netherlands were the pioneers in observing daily life and uplifting it into art. As a kid I felt spoken to by these works and connected with what it was that drove the artists to do their work. I never lost that connection. I believe it was not so much the subject matter, but more the mastery, the vision and the whole artist's enterprise that took hold of me then. It was also where I got the fascination with visual alchemy, the process of transformation, turning the base material of everyday life, the so-called "facts" into inspired meaning.

CHAPTER FIFTEEN
The Rest of Society

For most of us, knowing who we are is not an immediate knowing but a drawn-out process of becoming aware and it is never finished. It is an awareness composed of many small points of enlightenment accumulated over the years, finally solidifying into an overriding realization. We do not "make" ourselves so much as we "happen to ourselves" as Carl Jung asserts. As we mature into adulthood, we get drawn into all the latest preoccupations of society, the thoughts most people, swept up in the current of ideas of the time favor, the so-called "Zeitgeist," the spirit of the times. Modern life is very complicated with its ever-accelerating pace of change. It offers many ways to distract us from knowing ourselves, and many ways to barricade our natural intuitions behind walls of fashionable and supposedly undeniable truths. Marshall McLuhan's observation "There are many people for whom thinking necessarily means identifying with existing trends," as mentioned before is spot on. What he is saying is that few of us have our own thoughts. Having your own thoughts takes work, and it is part of the required "mastery" of the True Artist. The True Artist is not and cannot be a follower. The True Artist is also aware, often painfully so, that he cannot step outside of his own times and is locked in them. This idea is beautifully described by Ortega Y Gasset in his book

CHAPTER FIFTEEN

"*The Revolt of the Masses*," where it was first brought to my attention. He gave expression to vague feelings I had harbored for a long time but considered strange and immature.

While fighting your way through years of doubt and miscalculations, you are in the process of fashioning your being in accordance with your deepest, truest impulses. This realization dawns on you now and then, and then gets lost again in the jumble of daily preoccupations, to pop up sometime later. We can congratulate ourselves if we have the good fortune of living in a society that gives us freedom to work through it all, but for those who do not, the task is even more sharply delineated. The True Artist always has a fight on his or her hands trying to escape to freedom. It may often be a quiet, less than obvious struggle, but it can also be a very definite and more outward struggle opposing forces that always lie in wait to take control of our lives. This opposition of the world can become productive of great depth in the work of the True Artist. Growing our own inner awareness of our destiny comes through the many victories and defeats we have in this struggle.

As related before, one of those small victories came to me in an unlikely place and in an unexpected way in the so-called "fashion district" in downtown Los Angeles. It was just around the corner from the Orpheum movie theater, one of the iconic movie palaces still intact from the era of grand movie palaces. This is the theater film makers use whenever they want to make a movie about the glory days of Hollywood. A few steps from there, in a nondescript office space we were busy creating fabric designs. Nothing highfalutin, but rather common but well-selling ones. The craft I learned craft from it made me comfortable with painting with gouache which I could eventually use for illustration work for productions of A&E and the History

Channel. This was way before it all got taken over by computers. To counter the critical voice that kept harassing me at that time about being "just someone who painted fabric designs," I could have learned psychological strategies from a therapist to get rid of it, but it was, in its own nasty way my destiny trying to get my attention! I did not see it that way, and I doubt a therapist could have seen it for me, and it came out more as bemoaning my fate and my failure to live up to something that I was not even sure of! I received some affirmation through the work, because it was at least creative work, the big challenge for someone like me (and you!) of working in the commercial sphere is that it is easy to get permanently stuck there. It can be the comfort of good pay (it wasn't!) or a lack of moral courage, but when you stay with it, you may wake up years later and wonder what happened to your original intentions.

There were all these different interests I had that seemed to go off in all kinds of different directions and made me doubt whether there was a core to all of this, any coherence. Now, I can say with confidence to my younger self, "do not worry, there *is*, and all the things flying off in different directions will somehow, miraculously it seems, prove to be part of a coherent pattern; your inner guidance mechanism is not defective. It is intact, but you must learn to listen to it, recognize its voice and pay heed to it." What I have come to call the "True Artist control center" is always operating. All the things you are naturally interested in, even the things you may feel are inconsequential, are most likely part of the pattern of your destiny unfolding. All the scattered puzzle pieces and how they fit together sometimes shows us gentle confrontations with life, sometimes harsher ones. The confrontation in the Los Angeles fashion district came gently at a lunch break.

CHAPTER FIFTEEN

It came by way of those few lines by a poet whose identity would remain hidden from me for many years. Only when search engines became sophisticated enough to make a search possible would I know who he was. When I came across his work I could not then finish the poem nor find the poet's name, because I got my sandwich handed to me, but these lines became edged in my mind with a fine engraving needle, and eventually got me on a treasure hunt over all those years, several decades really. They had an incredible indelible force. I can never forget it. Poetry can do that. There was an immediate connection with the poet.

Two lines only, they were however an answer to my inner impasse. The light went on—I no longer was just a misplaced fabric designer, I was an artist who was "doing fabric designs." It was also a resounding refutation of all the unsolicited good advice I had been given throughout my life by well-meaning people, most likely in response to my unhappiness. This poet, however, seemed to understand me perfectly, and restored me to myself. And I felt I understood him perfectly, and a bond was created between us, as good poetry can do, and one that would expand over the years in significant ways, as I will show later.

Mani's line said that "Yes!", I could be whatever I wanted to be, a shoe cobbler of any kind, a fabric designer, a museum guard and yet be on the path, the path of destiny of a True Artist. In him I found someone in the world who understood my way of being, and had spoken to me, and given me courage. In fact, I can say in all honesty: indomitable strength and staying power, because no matter the challenges I faced, I would always remember Mani's lines. Everything I did from that point on was guided by that insight. Thank you, Mani Leib! We will return to his poem in full later, because it deserves more attention, there are more treasures in it.

"Poets deal in truths different from facts," S. H. Butcher in his comments on Aristotle's "Poetics." Poetry goes beyond fact, transcends it. What are the so-called "facts" anyway? What makes a fact, a fact? What makes it true? Without getting into treacherous philosophical swamplands best left to philosophers, we can claim that it is the artists among us that deal in truths of which facts are the mere bare bones. The truth of life is the meat we put on those bones, it is in the meaning we give it, and that is what True Artists do; that is the flame of culture they tend. Our modern obsession with facts makes life feel more like a court case, or a television police drama, like the long running television show "Dragnet" from which we get the iconic phrase: "Just the facts, ma'am!" Art lifts us above fact, the trivial. Our thoughts about things too, are mere encrustations of our real experience. The meaning of life is fashioned by True Artists, who wrestle from the facts a certain poetry.

The poet is the one who takes on the elements of life and submits them to a process of linguistic or visual transformation; meaning is wrestled from the immediacy of experience. The poet uses common words and phrases, the ones we use in daily life, but does so in a way that reveals a larger, deeper meaning. This is a most apt definition of the True Artist's task; using everyday reality to reveal an inner greatness hidden in its very ordinariness. It is what we see in Vermeer's work, or a more contemporary artist like Edward Hopper. To have this greater meaning revealed to us is what makes us want to live and have the strength to persevere in life.

CHAPTER SIXTEEN

Exile

Starting in my student days, I would go home every year for the Christmas holidays for a week or so. Though flying was cheap, my parents helped with the fare, which was fortunate for I did not have much money. On one of those trips, I had a conversation with my father that was hard to forget and became one of the mental "attic treasures" of which we will speak later. It was not an easy conversation. I was in my early to mid-twenties and our relationship was strained. He was most likely disappointed that I was throwing away the good education he felt he had given me. I understand his point of view now very well. Thankfully our relationship would grow into maturity and ease later, but it was quite strained at that time, as it had been while growing up. Of course, he would ask the inevitable question whenever we saw each other, "…and how are things going?" If I had been ruthlessly honest, I would have told him, "I am quite confused, because I am not sure of what I am doing, what my life is all about. I am hanging in there, but not happily." And, I could have added, that "despite it all, I do not want to go back!" Yes, I had had several decent jobs (by a parent's measurement), I was taking drawing and painting lessons, and seriously committed there. I had made my apartment into some manner of studio, but I was no good by my own standards. I existed on the vapors of romantic dreams of one day getting good. I knew that all this was not what he had envisioned for me, and certainly not what I had been educated for. Being honest in my self-evaluation would not have been what a father would want to hear. I am not even sure that I was aware enough to have given such a reasonable perspective on my own life then. When you are in the middle of the swamplands of the soul, as psychologist James Hollis calls them, it is hard to have a good perspective on things. My father had had high hopes for me and was proud when he saw me off at the boat that would take me to "America!" – the place of limitless possibilities – as it was always seen by many successive generations. I felt that my honest answer was not what he wanted to hear in response to his question; maybe I should have just risked it, but I did not and went for the other option – be real and try to connect on a deeper level. Without getting into any of the details (which were not glorious), I said, in all honesty, "I feel somewhat like I am in exile!" This was close to how I really felt, how life felt to me, and what Ezra Pound spoke of in the last line of his poem "The Rest," mentioned before. Without hesitation my father shot back in the kind of flash of disappointed frustration he had exhibited many times before, "The Jews in Egypt were in exile, *you* are *not* in exile!"

I got his point. What he meant was you are lucky just to have what you have, having been able to study "abroad," having had all these opportunities, and I do not want to hear about how much you are suffering! The life his son was living was, to his mind, one of ease and comfort. It was not, but he did not know that. I felt ashamed, but the reality of the situation was that I had been very honest. The truth was that I *did* feel like I was in exile. But of course, for exile to be genuine it cannot be self-chosen; you are forced into it

CHAPTER SIXTEEN

by powers beyond your control. My exile was self-chosen, though I really felt at that time that I had no other option. It was a proper decision although a painful one, even with all the glory attached to it. Exile was an ancient form of punishment. To be banished from your country, your kinsmen, your city of birth, your family, was a greater punishment than we cannot really understand in a time of easy travel and communications. Yet some of the best and wisest humanity ever produced have been driven into exile by those in power. Great ones, like Cicero, one of history's most excellent statesmen and thinkers, had been driven into exile for no other reason than his peers, those in power, knowing themselves to be his inferiors intellectually, spiritually, and creatively, had forced him out of their "club." Being a man of rare brilliance, he would point out the folly of their actions. Being brilliant is not something that is easily tolerated by those less gifted. This is a common theme in human history. But for me, being neither brilliant nor in power, I was indeed not in exile!

Nevertheless, I was! It is important to recognize my own truth even though it is hard to admit to. It took years to see things more clearly. I should have said, "I simply could not be myself while I was here, close to you guys, I was forced to leave, and my chance to qualify for an exchange program was the best chance I felt I had, and I took it. If the exchange program had been with some place in the Sahara Desert, I would have gone there." Of course, I felt guilty; what kind of ungrateful son-of-a-gun was I, and how self-aggrandizing, seeing myself in exile, while I was not? My father had had to flee from the Nazis who were ever more squeezing him and his family's life and well-being, slowly suffocating them, making laws that targeted them as outlaws. He had to adopt a new country, a new culture, very different from what he had grown up in. Germany and The Netherlands may be bordering each other and to the American mind may look similar, but they are worlds apart, cultures apart, even now. Indeed, he would have had a right to say he was in exile, but he never did. To hear his son say he was in exile, while he pictured me as having a golden life in the glittering US, must have been galling to him. Only much later did I learn that I was actually living my father's dream, and that his original intention was to flee to the US, but he had gotten "stuck" in The Netherlands when he fell for that beautiful Dutch blonde, my mother.

So yes, I did feel "in exile," that much was true. Now I can see where that feeling originated. The true exile was my exile from my True Artist destiny that was stirring in me. Of course, I would have never been able to identify it as such at the time. As it was, I just felt like an ungrateful young man, not deserving of what I got. But it is not what you have that is important. I would have felt in exile in paradise on earth had I been able to go there. The exile that I was in was more difficult to identify and would necessarily lead to a lot of perilous detours and missteps.

The world does not understand, and cannot understand, and will not understand, and is not required to understand, that you are one who is burdened and gifted with the inner directive to be a True Artist and nothing else. It is a storm that must be weathered, as Pound says, an "exile to be beaten out." It is work, and no amount of feeling "special" and "mistrusted" and "spoken against" is going to save you from having to save yourself, saving that which is the most beautiful thing that was installed in your inner being. You may consider yourself one of the "finer sense," you may feel "hated," "shut in," and "mistrusted," (see pages 83/84) but that does not give you a special exemption from something that the world cannot know about until you yourself are able to give it form. It is a definite characteristic of the True Artist that he "can only speak," and "know at first hand." That is the great gift we are given if we have that special call, but it is not something that I can pride myself on having, other than taking up the fight to bring it to fruition. That is the real "finer sense" you have. I must take direct aim at some of the sentiment expressed in the poem. It is not true that you are "helpless against the control," it is not true that you are "broken" against some outside force. You may be lost in the villages, and the town, and especially the big modern cities, but you *can* beat out your exile—the poet says so himself—because that is the very essence of the life that is meant for you.

If you feel different from your fellows and they do not agree with you and oppose you, be vigilant and see if you truly believe in what you are saying and doing or if you are just being reactive. If you find in your heart that you truly believe what you are saying you believe, then stick with what you know. If you get into too much trouble with others for expressing it, store that away, put it in a notebook with date and place of the writing, and remind yourself that ultimately it will have to come out in the work you do. There is work involved here. There is mastery involved here. There is the transformation of poetics involved here. When you feel that your judgment is not wanted, that does not make your judgment invalid. People do not like it when what they believe is not confirmed in a conversation. The real conversation with them takes place when you do your work and become part of a band of culture builders, the so-called "keepers of the flame." That is where the True Artist makes his mark, presses her point.

The discipline of depth psychology, with its emphasis on the unconscious, has proven beyond a doubt that we are emotionally driven, and as Jung's followers would call it, image driven. The creators of the image shape and stimulate our behavior, and much more than we are willing to admit. Not just our fantasies or dreams, but our actual behavior in the world. By "image" we mean to indicate something much wider than just a picture. An image, in the depth psychological sense we use it here, is a cluster of intricately connected meanings and intentions evoking focused passions in ways we are not rationally in control of. A great painting can be such an image, and that would count as a "picture," but it is a picture where several dimensions are present at the same time. An image can then just as well be evoked by poetry or music. When we are listening to music, we may see interior images, and those will be the intention of the musician coming together with our own inner landscape of images, our hopes, dreams, and fantasies. A dream image, though coming from our own inner being and fugitive as it may be, is also such a multi-dimensional image. It takes some doing, but when we do the work, and give it its own time to unfold, its inner coherence will be revealed.

The True Artist works in the field of those kinds of images. Some may be direct and seem rather unambiguous, but the true image stays with you and unfolds within you long after you have experienced it; that is serving the collective purposes of society. Without that, people are lost.

CHAPTER SEVENTEEN
Genius, Talent, Resentment, Depression

We have been dealing with questions that plague many True Artist types—Do I have what it takes? How do I know for sure? Now we must shed more light on the issues of talent, genius, and their relation to a True Artist's destiny. Western culture's obsession with genius has been replaced for a large part with the obsession with fame, but the issue has not gone away. The subject of genius is hard to address in a time when we want to make everyone feel equally good about themselves. However, the fact remains that there are those who stand out and ignoring that does not make it go away. Genius is real. A great way to deal with these issues is to look at the life of Mozart, one of the world's greatest composers. Looking at him gives us some insight about talent, genius, and how we ordinary mortals stack up. Ever since the Renaissance there has been this Western cultural preoccupation with "genius." Before that, both in the West and the East, there was little emphasis on the creators of art. They were often even anonymous, something that we find hard to imagine as the inheritors of the obsession with genius which has now morphed into this obsession with fame.

A first indication of genius is that Mozart's music is loved by millions of people from very different cultural backgrounds than his. By that fact alone, we know we are in the presence of something special. To reach that many very diverse people over such a long time is a sign of genius indeed. Genius connects with a vast inner realm of imagination that is common to us all. What psychologists indicate as the collective unconscious is that place where we all meet in our humanness. Genius is the ability to tap into that vast reservoir of meaning and intention which is part of our natural inheritance. When you look up the word genius in the dictionary, it talks mostly about intelligence and ability because it cannot describe that special connection to something infinitely greater that we find in someone like Mozart. There are many other great ones we could look at, but Mozart gives us a great opportunity to sort things out a bit, especially since a very accessible piece of movie art was made around his life.

Mozart had a natural, uncomplicated connection with the poetic imagination, which is ultimately the essence of music and theater, and above all, being human. To give form to his insight he had the other important element of the True Artist: mastery! His mastery was of an organic nature, but his talent was also disciplined and harnessed by growing up with a father who was one of the great musicians of his time. Genius is where the parts that go into the making of the True Artist—destiny, mastery, poetics and the discipline needed—come together in a commanding way. Mozart was no tender green house plant but stood fully in life, full of zest and of a decidedly bawdy disposition. Side by side with the loftiness of his religious music, he also engaged in a "naughty" composition he titled "Kiss my *ss;" not something we would consider high culture, but maybe we should.

The renowned British psychiatrist Anthony Storr proposed a "genius continuum" running from Mozart to

Beethoven. He juxtaposed their ways of creating by putting Mozart at one pole of the continuum and Beethoven at the other. Mozart would write down music which he had composed "in his head," and then put down pretty much the way he "heard" it, and as it was "supposed" to be. It seems being continuously on the road in a horse drawn carriage, with its rhythmic rattling of the wheels (which we still experience in a train ride), set his creative juices flowing. And it seemed to come out nearly perfect. Beethoven, occupying the opposite pole, was an indefatigable laborer. He would map out his compositions in sketch after sketch, working from clunky to superb, by laborious corrections and revisioning of the work, until he felt satisfied. Compared to Mozart, Beethoven was a plotter. Though Mozart also sketched out his compositions, compared to Beethoven, his way of composing was like a natural flow. Both are rightfully considered certified geniuses though; the passage of time has confirmed that. Most of us are closer to the Beethoven side of the continuum. The fascination with child prodigies, for whom things just seem to come naturally, is part of our obsession with the genius dimension of things. All aspiring artists must wrestle with the genius dimension of things, it is part of the territory.

I told my students once that it was a great day for me when I gave up on being a genius. The effort of trying to prove to myself that I was had exhausted itself. A new freedom set in. The students would look at me puzzled, almost disbelieving. I thought I understood where that puzzlement came from. As aspiring artists, they must entertain the notion that they very well might be a genius, who knows, and they must find out. But there is no way of concocting genius, it is there, or it is not. All we can do is tease out where our genius lies, because though few *are* geniuses, many of us have some genius somewhere, and finding out where that may be is of great importance.

Playwright Peter Shaeffer wrote a play called "Amadeus" in which he uses some facts of Mozart's life (1756-1791) to throw light on these complicated matters. As a playwright he takes poetic license to increase the dramatic effect, but he does so to make a larger point about the relationship of genius and talent. Russian playwright Alexander Pushkin had done this before Shaeffer, in a play called "Mozart and Salieri." Both plays focus on the relationship between Mozart and one of his contemporaries, composer Salieri.

A movie well worth your time was made of the play. It is highly entertaining, profound, thought provoking, and inspiring—like all good art. Additionally, the soundtrack is a surefire hit as it uses Mozart's own music. The story is about Wolfgang Amadeus seen from the viewpoint of Antonio Salieri. The raw material of their lives, the so-called facts, are by means of poetics, recast to reveal greater truths. The meta facts which the playwright means to bring out, remain the same for all time. How the story unfolds gives us some of the "suggestive hints" by which we try to get at the *True Artist's Destiny*.

The story is as follows. Salieri, a very accomplished composer, has risen to the enviable position of court composer, at the very center of power of one of the great empires of Europe, the Austro-Hungarian Empire (1867-1918). He is employed at the court of Emperor Josef II in Vienna, the capital. Since being a composer always has been and still is a rather tenuous position in society, the position that Salieri has at this court is about as powerful as you could get. At the conclusion of World War I, the Austro-Hungarian Empire collapses into the small country we now know as Austria, a shadow of its former self, with Vienna remaining as its

CHAPTER SEVENTEEN

capital, and still showing the grandeur of its past, but before that time it is one of the great empires of Europe.

Salieri has achieved a most enviable position for any musician at that time. Mozart, younger than Salieri, is a rising musical star but in comparison to Salieri, a musician without a steady gig so to speak. He is making his mark though, incessantly traveling around Europe. The story as told, shows us that Salieri recognizes Mozart's special gift, something that he feels he lacks, setting up the sense of envy we see often among artists. Mozart is scheduled to give a concert at the court and Salieri is eager to meet this mysterious composer. Having never met Mozart—no television, no social media, no FaceTime, no video, no newspaper photos even—he is eager to see what kind of person this special composer might be.

On the day of the concert, all the nobility as well as the power elite of the church are gathered in the palace, dressed in their finery, making appropriate small talk. In the movie you see Salieri wandering through this crowd of fashionably dressed young women and men, wondering if he can spot a special man like Mozart just by looks. What does a genius like that look like? Can you read the power from the outside? Is there a special sign, a special indication somewhere, on his face, in his demeanor? Looking at the crowd, he wonders as he mills through the crowd—could that young man there be Mozart? Or maybe that one?

Not able to come to any conclusions he goes into an anteroom of which the door is open, and there finds the tables laden with fancy food trays to be brought out after the concert. He stealthily tastes one of the delicacies when a young woman comes rushing into the room shrieking loudly while giggling; she does not see him. She dives unceremoniously under one of the tables with food, as if trying to hide from someone. Salieri is a bit taken aback by this unceremonious behavior not quite befitting a grand palace. He hides behind some of the extravagant food displays and from this hiding place he sees a curious scene unfolding. He sees the legs of a young man entering the room and calling out to the girl. The young man then dives under the table as well, laughing, and grabs the girl by her legs, dragging her out from under the table. Though protesting, she does it with a charming giggle that shows she somehow enjoys the play. When finally sitting together on the floor they start to talk. At first it is just silly talk, and the young man seems a bit oafish, a bit vulgar really, in the way he treats the young woman, especially in a place of high protocol as the imperial palace. It is all in good fun though. Then their innocent play becomes somewhat more overtly sexual, and they start to make out a bit. Salieri, ever the proper courtier, seems properly scandalized, but also intrigued, voyeuristically enjoying their sensual play. The young people think they are alone, and do not know they are being observed. Then a pivotal moment in the story arrives with a bang.

At some point the young man suddenly freezes and scrambles to his feet as if startled by something. We hear distant music playing. Alarmed, the young man blurts out, "They started without me!" He stands up and adds, "They are playing my music!!" As the young man runs out the door adjusting his disheveled clothes and wig, we see Salieri's face totally bewildered, his eyes popping out of their sockets. "That was Mozart!!" Salieri blurts out in obvious disgust and bitterness. By this time the movie scene has shifted, and we see Salieri as an old man talking to a young priest, relating the episode we just saw. It becomes clear that he is by now in an insane asylum reminiscing to the young priest, who can barely handle the ferocity of Salieri's utterances.

CHAPTER SEVENTEEN

In the way Peter Shaeffer tells the story we are given to think about the issues of talent versus genius, the power and glory of art versus worldly power, the gremlins of envy and resentment, and its relation to depression and madness. How Salieri ends up in an insane asylum is an important part of the story. According to the story as presented, Salieri has had a lifelong obsession with becoming a great composer, an immortal one perhaps. His prayers were about being granted musical genius. What he got was fame and prestige and power. He seems to have sacrificed all that makes life wonderful to achieve all this. Now he is confronted with this boorish kid, coarse and unrefined, and this kid is what he is not, but has always longed to be—a musical genius! This sets up the tension in Salieri that becomes his undoing.

But all that is "psychologizing," and while that has its importance, it is also just the surface layer of the story. Most of life is trying to break through that surface layer of life, the day-to-day, the obvious, and get to the innate truth of who we are, which we can indicate with the word 'genius'. Being a genius is different from having genius. In my estimation, all of us *have* it. The origins of the word genius are very revealing. Originally from Latin, it means "attendant spirit present from one's birth" and "innate ability or inclination." In the 17th century it morphed from "natural ability" to "exceptional natural ability." That is where the problem started because we confuse innate ability with being exceptional. By definition, not everyone can be exceptional, so the original meaning of "innate ability," as something that is with us "from birth," spontaneous to us, unlearned, "in the blood," is what we mean here.

The essential meaning being unveiled in this story—and many other stories like it—is that we, like Salieri, look for that own inner genius in all the wrong places. We confuse innate ability with exceptional ability. We can understand things properly by means of this story. Salieri, going through the fashionably dressed and properly behaving crowd gathered at the palace, searching for the genius Mozart, cannot find him. Genius seems not so easily identified just by looking, just by outward signs. In fact, it is found unexpectedly in an anteroom of the fancy palace. That it is the one with the food, is also metaphorically significant in that food is one of the basic ingredients of life, no matter how fancily displayed. Genius is what bursts into that room of basic ingredients, fashionably displayed and has an unfashionable appearance. Genius turns out to be the lout, boorish, uncouth. Genius surprises us as it is not as expected or desired at all.

That inner genius we are always looking to find, like Salieri going through the elite crowd, is not found in the fancy places among the fashionably dressed parts of us, the way we like to present ourselves to the world and to ourselves. We find it in the places we often look upon with disdain, the parts of us we believe unacceptable to the eyes of the world. Yet there it is! That part of us, unfashionably dressed, surprises us with its un-genius appearance, simple and instinctive, yet it is, after all, the true genius of us. We may have been looking to prestigious art academies, famous teachers, "cool" contemporaries, but find it in the parts of ourselves we have often disapproved of!

Besides having taught young students, I have worked with many adult students as well. Some of these were art teachers themselves and several were retired. For both groups the same issues are important, but they become more pertinent when we have reached full maturity. The latter are further removed from a direct connection with the real self, which is more possible when we are young even if we are not fully conscious of it. More mature students have built up an entire repertoire of sophisticated opinions about art and what is good art in their view. From this arises their desire for being a certain kind of artist or doing a certain type of art. Their sophistication has become a barrier between them and their genius dimension within. That genius part of us often goes hidden in the rejected part of ourselves, those parts we have found to be unacceptable. The more sophisticated we become, the more that rejection of the "raw" aspects of the self has been solidified and the harder it is to access them. Those raw aspects also include the connection with that destiny point of our being. While accessing that destiny is by no means impossible, there is usually a great sense of relief when the connection is made, as if the key to greater creativity has been finally found.

Many great actors in Hollywood had to make way for a less great actor whose aura just translated better to the screen, one who had an instinctive bond with the movie camera and an organic connection to their own genius-dimension. Actors, like other artists, are a very competitive lot and this may breed resentments in those who are, like Salieri, struggling to find that connection. Resentments are the products of the rational mind and the big plans it has for us, coming in collision with who we really are. The tension between how we want to be perceived by the world, how we feel we ought to be, and who we really are, can get so intense that we resolve it either through addiction of some sort, depression (we are "de-pressing" our real self), or like in the movie, by going mad, which means that irrationality triumphs over the ego. Our natural destiny may not be of the glorious heights that we have dreamed of for ourselves, but it is ours and no one else's. Ancient Vedic literature speaks of the hazards of assuming someone else's dharma (destiny) rather than one's own. It warns us that we may even be able to do someone else's dharma better than they themselves could, but that it puts us in "spiritual danger" to do so.

For the True Artist, experiencing that emotional strain, that aching pain, can be seen as a warning that there is a tension in our being that demands our attention and requires resolution. The ego may rebel mightily, but the work demands to be done. The songwriter who should be doing country songs but is aiming at being a classical soloist is setting up that inner antagonism, leading him or her out of harmony with the self. There is a high price to be paid for not recognizing one's own gifts, one's own innate ability. It is often when confronted with a superior talent that we get shocked into the reality of our own being. It is by these "collisions" with reality, as Jung calls them, that our true nature takes on its proper shape. They are not to be avoided; they are our friends in the end, if properly understood and acted upon. Overcoming the initial shock of that confrontation, then making proper adjustments, is an important part of the work of the True Artist, more so than with most other paths in life. The True Artist must work from who they really are, and that is what a Mozart-like genius is so eminently capable of.

Few composers, few artists if any, have the Mozart ability. But many of us have the ability to create from the true dimension of our being, from within our own "dharma." True genius is so rare that we are still talking about Mozart centuries later as if no other great composers have come along since him. Ultimately time decides who is and who is not a genius. The ultimate issue is: does the art speak to us? Mozart's work does and has been doing so for centuries. With all his innate talents, highly refined proficiency and ultimate mastery, his greatest ability was to connect with the basic ingredients of all life. It was not until somewhat later in life that I could see how his work reaches into the highest spiritual realm as well as the most human, instinctual sides of us. The music historian Federico Cortese, commenting on Mozart's genius, gives us a True Artist angle on it when he says,

> "One of the most extraordinarily impressive things about him is how he could understand the corners of human feelings, even at a rather young age. He must have been hypersensitive and therefore emotionally very vulnerable: certainly, very aware of everything that was going on around him."

Mozart did not shy from subject matter that his age considered beneath its dignity and the high aspirations of art. He startled the sophisticates by creating, for example, an opera dealing with a harem, considered a lowly subject matter. By way of his mastery, he turned this spicy subject matter into immortal art. To his mind it was highly entertaining and exciting. Mozart was a fun-loving lusty guy, gifted with talent and the compensatory discipline to turn it into heavenly music. He understood love and spirituality, romance and lust. As a True Artist, he knew how to transform the ingredients of normal life into great art. He achieved mastery from a very young age, greatly helped by his father of course. Trained by him, chaperoned by him, guided by him, Mozart could be himself. Playing for the French king at age six then composing a first opera at the age of twelve, things lined up for him in a way that is not given to most.

Many who were once considered great are now forgotten. This is how it is and should be. What is considered exceptional in one era is not so in another. Yet there are a few, and only a few, who transcend their own specific era and remain exceptional for all times. But all this does not really matter. True Artists may not be celebrated, yet they have an impact on the world around them, which is important to the life of society, allowing people to live together in their own times.

This whole drama of fame, genius, the spirit of the times, and posterity, is made visible in amazing ways in that world famous, quintessentially romantic cemetery in Paris, France, called Père Lachaise. It is one of the most famous cemeteries in the world because many famous people are buried there. It is filled with large, impressive monuments erected to once highly esteemed people, and yet we pass by them wondering: who was *that*? Additionally, there are many small seemingly forgotten graves and mausoleums which make for quaint narrow alleyways. Some simple gravesites are strewn with flowers every day. Those are the graves of those who spoke to the many. One of those graves is the grave of another immortal composer, Chopin, whose music is familiar to many who may not know his name but have heard his music in many movie soundtracks. His is a simple grave, not demanding any outsized attention. It has a small sculpture of an angel sitting in a slumped-over, dejected pose with a harp that has almost slipped from her hands. It always has many flowers while the big commanding monuments for once important power players stand barren. There is the grave of Jim Morrison, singer of the rock band The Doors, where there is always a spectacle of onlookers. It is also interesting to know that his grave has been vandalized many times so people could take pieces of it home. They had to rebuild it in a non-exciting way; it is rather standard and unremarkable now. Morrison's legacy may not last as long as Chopin's, but for now he may well outdraw Chopin and many of the other greats buried there. This is a great

CHAPTER SEVENTEEN

commentary on the flickering flame of fame and the stage of our civilization. Just for the record, I do like the music of The Doors and understand how Jim Morrison was one of those special charismatic individuals on which pop culture thrives and which draws people to him even in death.

There is also a grave not that well-known which, in a wonderful way, brought me unexpected companionship. It lit up an essential dimension of the True Artist destiny in a totally unexpected way, worthy of a scene in a movie. It is the grave of Gustav Doré. Though not known to many, he was a pivotal artist and made innovations that are with us today. Unlike the flash and glare of rock legends like Jim Morrison (who ended up at Père Lachaise because he happened to be staying in Paris at the time of his untimely death), Doré's is a kindly light, a soft one which penetrates with force to the essence of things, which is something a True Artist aims at. Though well-known in professional circles, Gustave Doré (1832-1883) is not a household name like Mozart. My experience with his grave at Père Lachaise brought to light the special connections that True Artists forge through their work. This is one of the suggestive hints with which the souls of ripening True Artists are seeded.

Doré was one of the most wildly productive and gifted illustrators ever; he was also a painter, sculptor, printmaker, and comics artist. He was as natural a genius as Mozart. His illustrations for major literary works are very familiar to many, without them knowing who made them. His images are most often used without attribution, which is a startling thing to contemplate. His work for Dante's *Divine Comedy*, Milton's *Paradise Lost*, Cervantes' *Don Quixote*, ancient mythology, and his magnificent illustrations for the Bible, remain unequalled. He is well-known to moviemakers, production designers, and art directors. When you see his work, for example, a book on the Crusades, you know where the battle scenes in the movie of "The Lord of the Rings" most likely come from. His work on fantasy creatures, monsters, demons, and dragons rivals anything done today, and are a rich resource for today's comics artists. Superlative stuff, all of it. His very large paintings on display in London are amazing as well. How he crammed so much work in such a short life is mind-boggling.

Back to Paris and Père Lachaise. My spouse and I wanted to visit Doré's grave since both of us love his work. The cemetery is very confusing and besides the more well laid out lanes, has a rather hop-scotch configuration. We had to buy a special map showing where all the graves are located. We walked shady lanes and little streets lined with small mausoleums, tombs, monuments, and crumbling gravestones upended by gnarly roots of ancient looking chestnut trees, making it hard to walk in places. Even with map in hand it was hard to find his grave, somewhat hidden behind some trees and bushes. We could not find it at first and it began to feel like a treasure hunt. And that is exactly what it turned out to be for us. The grave itself is rather unassuming, an above-ground sarcophagus and not exactly imposing. The cemetery is indeed a romantic's dream of a graveyard, complete with the quality of ruin and chaos.

When we finally got to the grave it did not stand out from the graves around it and looked rather unkempt. After cleaning off some of the debris, twigs, and leaves on top, we decided to come back the next day and put a rose on it as a tribute, to pay homage to an artist who meant a lot to both of us. The next day we came back and brought a single rose. We made our way back to the grave in the early afternoon (it was still difficult to find again). When we got there, we were stunned to find a single red rose on the grave!

CHAPTER SEVENTEEN

Someone had had the exact same idea, and at exactly the same time it seemed, someone who wanted to honor this artist as we did. It took my breath away. In that moment we felt a special connection to some unknown member of the secret brotherhood of True Artists. We connected without knowing each other and in all its obscurity it was a truly meaningful encounter; it affirmed our destiny and our own dedication to our art. To me, this was a meeting of the secret brotherhood! A great moment without flash, but with deep meaning. Perhaps this is how the secret brotherhood meets after all.

CHAPTER EIGHTEEN
Do True Artists Make Good Art?

Truth is lived, not taught.

—Hermann Hesse

Does being a True Artist translate into making good art? It is a natural question, but it misses the point. Good art is quite simply an essential part of being a True Artist. There is no such thing as a True Artist without mastery, and mastery holds a lot of meaning for us. Good art is always possible, but the good art of a True Artist is necessarily of a different order than the good art of just any proficient artist, because mastery is proficiency carried to a next level. Being a masterful artist is just the outer layer of being a True Artist. A True Artist is capable of doing the work necessary to reach into the soul of another. Whether something is good or not is not for some elite to decide. The elites, such as there are, have often been proven wrong in their judgment because they are players in a power game which is usually alien to the True Artist. The True Artist remains faithful to a goal which seeks its own audience and aims to satisfy aspirations wider than solely those from the artist's ego.

CHAPTER EIGHTEEN

It is important to realize that there are creative artists who do work that many True Artists are not capable of. I have encountered many. I remember a seminar given by one of the grand masters of matte painting Albert "Al" Whitlock, before computer generated matte paintings became standard. Matte paintings are used in movie making to allow the movie maker to create settings which would otherwise be difficult or impossible to realize. At that time, they were actual paintings done with paint and brush and were meant to blend seamlessly with live film footage shot with it. They completely change the environment in which the live action is taking place. Matte paintings created some of the fantasy environments for movies like *Star Wars*, and many natural environments where a studio backlot is transformed into a metropolis at night. The magic was accomplished with actual paint on large glass panels, with a part left clear for the live shot to fit in. The color, the lighting, and the perspective had to exactly fit the live action and Whitlock was an expert at that. His knowledge of perspective, natural light effects on different surfaces, was amazing. The paintings he made looked very much like superb Impressionist paintings. The way they were painted was another part of his amazing expertise. He understood exactly how the camera saw things, which is not as straight forward as it seems. He painted what many would call "impressionistically" with suggestive brushstrokes and not like the photorealism of today's computer-generated matte paintings. Wondrously, this translated to the screen as fully realistic and believable. In-person these paintings were beautiful art, partly due to his incredible brushwork, except that they were paintings with a part missing, the empty spot of clear glass for the live action. I would have given anything at that time to be able to paint like that. I felt a bit like Salvador Dali who was supposed to have said that he would give his left hand to be able to see Vermeer paint and to know what he did to achieve his effects. After one of Al Whitlock's lectures, I went up to him and asked him what kind of work he enjoyed doing in his own studio at home. This was important for me to know, something I always wanted to know from any teachers I had. I was stunned by his answer! "When I am done here, that's it! No more painting for me!" I was floored and remember thinking something like: if I could only paint like you, I would be producing so much great stuff! Here I was in the presence of one of the greats of the movie industry. He was the brilliant super creative yet I, with less brilliance, was (and I knew it) the True Artist. That simply did not compute in my mind at the time! I learned a lot from him but there were things I apparently could not learn from him. I know it sounds conceited, but it is true! Only now do I understand why it was important for me to ask that question of him. My admiration for him was not diminished but I understood that there was a gulf between people like him and myself; something that I had to come to terms with.

When dealing with the question of the True Artists and good art, some examples come to mind. There are lots of them all over the world, but the ones I know best are familiar to enough people worldwide that I can safely use them. Again, there is the case of Van Gogh, who was famously unsuccessful both in making a living with his art and in getting any recognition. This seems to be part of his appeal in fact, and that tells us something about what is unconsciously prized, a tacit hat tip to the True Artist, as they live and work "astray and lost in the villages." Quite likely, Van Gogh's work was disparaged and found wanting by most people of that time, even the counter elite of the Impressionist crowd. This is a very difficult way to live, and it did not end well in

CHAPTER EIGHTEEN

the individual life of Vincent. But he was a True Artist and people from all over the world recognize it. Of course, so were Gauguin and Degas and Monet and they were able to make a living at it somehow and Monet even became famous rather late in life. Is Van Gogh's art "good?" Judging from the worldwide acceptance of his work, you would say it is; there seems to be no more universal acclaim for an artist than his, with the possible exception of Leonardo da Vinci. According to his contemporaries in general, his art was not good enough, but the succeeding generations have shown that his contemporaries were wrong.

This was confirmed when I visited a wonderful museum in my hometown of The Hague in the Netherlands. It was started by Anton Mesdag, a great painter himself. The museum is not as well-known as some of the other museums in the Netherlands and seems a bit forgotten almost. There is a reason for that, they told me. Mesdag was a good judge of art and collected master paintings, helped by the money he had made as a banker before a switch to art (the way Gauguin switched from finance to art). He bought up beautiful pieces from the so-called Barbizon School, which was a collection of artists named after the special nature preserve near Paris, Barbizon, which was where they went to paint their inspiring landscapes. Talking to some of the curatorial staff, I asked why the museum was not better known (for all the years I lived in The Hague as a young man I had not known about it!). I was told that if only Mesdag had seen the worth of Van Gogh and had bought just one piece, the museum would have been very popular! So, you see, not even the ones with a great eye, like this famous Dutch painter who started his own museum, saw the worth of a Van Gogh.

You can see a similar phenomenon happening in other creative fields. Frank Baum who is known as the author of

The Wonderful Wizard of Oz, was a True Artist as well. He wrote the books of which *The Wonderful Wizard of Oz* is just one, because he wanted to create American fairy tales, feeling that the German tales did not really fit the New World consciousness of America. He wanted to create what he called "American fairies." This means that he had a larger vision than just creating books and movies that sell. He wanted to create fairy tales that fit the American mind to tend to the soul of Americans, a new breed of citizen in the world.

Baum was, from what we know about him, a True Artist. I found out a lot about him when I dug into his creative life in some detail when tasked with designing an exhibit on his life and work for the Samuel Goldwyn Foundation in Los Angeles. Not only was his a vision larger than a businessman's intent, but he also had that special quality that marks remarkable artists. He was close to his creative child within, which is a hallmark of True Artists. You can observe a childlike joy when True Artists are doing their work. I was touched when I learned that the Oz stories originated in the bedtime stories his young sons insisted, he tell them. He said that as he was telling his boys these stories—made up on the spot—he felt more like one of them rather than their father. This moved me. It is what makes more seriously minded people disparage the True Artist's work as "mere play."

Baum went on to create, first his own theater company and then his own movie company. Eventually he made a movie out of his Wizard of Oz story, complete with special effects which still hold up and amaze, and for all their sophistication for that time have a childlike joy about them. You can also see how the eventual well-known commercial movie version, with Judy Garland as Dorothy, borrowed many ideas from that first version made by Baum. The

Hollywood movie, released in 1939, was not an immediate financial or critical success. Yet it became a perennial family film favorite when it was brought to television. Britannica online judges the movie as "culturally, historically, or aesthetically significant to film heritage." I would add to that that it was significant to the soul of society. Because of television, it became "a yearly staple" of generations growing up before streaming video. Through television, the film finally became that quintessential American fairy tale, and this was exactly what Baum had been aiming at all along. Baum was not there to see his vision realized, but his vision *was* very much realized! His characters became the "American fairies" he had envisioned. Vision carries a work to its true destination, though not always in a timely fashion. Vision is a hallmark of True Artists. They "see" where others do not see. They "speak directly," and "see at first hand," as Ezra Pound puts it in his poem.

Living the True Artist's life means perfecting your creative language of choice, lifting it up to serve your vision—the way you see life—and reporting on the living of it. To judge whether we are dealing with a True Artist on the merit of whether the work fits the appetites and tastes of a contemporary public or fits into the market would be a futile endeavor. Yet, we can certainly conclude whether a certain work connects with us on a deeper level and thus must have come from a deeper source, or whether it is made merely to entertain, delight, titillate, or divert us. Nothing is wrong with that. The True Artist's work can do all these things while at the same time connecting us with our deepest purposes of being alive. A True Artist's life may result in work that even the artist him—or herself may not be able to properly evaluate. Here we must exercise caution that we do not use this kind of reasoning to believe ourselves to be misunderstood geniuses beyond the grasp of our contemporaries, while actually not living up to our own true potential. A sense of dissatisfaction is better than a sense of intellectual or artistic superiority. As Michelangelo said, "The graver danger for most of us is not that our aim is too high and we miss it, but that it is too low, and we reach it." This is one of the things that makes the True Artist path not one of ease, but one of continual challenge. The satisfactions we derive from our work may not come often or may come when we least expect them. When they come though they are deep and lasting.

The wife of my mentor, as already mentioned. a wonderful artist in her own right, would say that good art "touches you in a place where you are not usually touched." That is a simple way of saying that good art is something deeply true and comes from wisdom gained in a lifelong engagement with the arts. Good art, to be good art, goes *to* a place that is hard to reach, because it *comes from* a place that is hard to reach. We must fight for being who we truly are, often against the prevailing winds of fashion and communal thought, which can seem like an opposing enemy. You cannot defeat an enemy if you think you do not have what it takes to do so. Therefore, while the term True Artist may feel a bit pretentious and self-congratulatory, it is neither of those things. It is a delicate balancing act, both a gentle touching and a warrior stance. The True Artist knows well enough that he or she has failed many times to do so, but what makes him or her a True Artist is that you have come back to fight again. Eventually the unconscious gets the message that you are indeed serious and in it for real! Then the misgivings and the trepidations back down. George Leonard, in his already mentioned book, and because he is an Aikido master, talks about how the master always shows

CHAPTER EIGHTEEN

up "on the mat" to do his practice, even if he is experiencing a dry spell, is on a plateau, or has felt no recent advancements in ability. He considers that the sign of a true master, not just in Aikido, but in general, is showing up every day to continue the work, even when there seems to be no advance for quite a while. Only the non-master would give up at a certain point and try something new to do. The master shows up regardless and practices.

CHAPTER NINETEEN

Vision

Vision is a hallmark of the True Artist. But what do we mean when we say that someone *has vision*? Of course, it has something to do with "seeing," but *vision* is different. We use it to say that someone has more than simple understanding or the power of observation. In the context of art, someone who has *vision* is more than being imaginative or perceptive, although it includes those things. Having vision means something almost entirely different. When someone with *vision* "sees" something he or she does not merely have thoughts or an idea about something but *sees* it fully and in its completeness. They see directly, without using the instrument of their eyes, like when we see things in our dreams without using eyes, yet definitely and clearly. Vision in the context of *having vision* is seeing without the use of your eyes but perceiving something in the totality of its presence. When you look at a mountain or a tree, you see the whole mountain, you see the whole tree, even though you do not see every crack in the rocks or every leaf on the tree. In the act of seeing, you are taking it all in, without taking all of it in. You are seeing it in the totality of its presence. This is materially different than having imagination. In imagining you are doing something. *Seeing* is not doing, it is *receiving* what is "out there," wherever that "out there" may be. We are receptive to what is presented to us, rather than actively and intentionally creating it. When we have vision we are dynamically receiving, not passively. Having vision for the True Artist is part of mastery. Since mastery is having such command of our means that we no longer have to think about how to use them; we can let our instincts take over. This command over our means is also what allows us to be responsive to that inner guidance—which we call having *vision*. Having a clever idea is not the same as having vision.

The subject of vision is very large and has been written about by many thinkers, artists, and authors. They have commented on the dark aspect of this most wonderful capacity, namely that people of vision are often found suspect by their contemporaries. The writer Herman Hesse even remarked that those who have vision are deemed "sinister" by those who do not share in their gift; it makes others uncomfortable. This negative side of things is so deeply engrained in the collective mindset that people who do have vision often discount or denigrate their own capacity; it challenges their contact with others. There is also the confusion around being a person of vision and a person *having visions*. Having visions lands us in the territory of the supernatural and that is not what we are talking about here. I dare say that many people *see* in the manner of having vision, but that they dismiss their own *seeing*. The saving grace for an artist of vision has always been the mastery they bring to the task of giving form, giving life, to what they see. Through mastery their seeing becomes concretized and taken out of the realm of speculation. Their art is the definite form their vision takes.

CHAPTER TWENTY
Modern Times and the Language of Dreams

> *The really modern man is often found among those who call themselves old-fashioned. In this way he dissociates himself from the pseudo-modern...who deny the past for the sake of being conscious of the present.*
>
> —V. W. Odajnyck.[1]

The times we live in are difficult in novel ways, and in ways that made someone say, "If you are not stumped, you are not paying attention!" Things move too fast for human beings to grasp, to catch up with. True Artists however, always live in their own time, and so must deal with the difficulty in a way that fits their vision, their direct seeing. The speed of change is what is new, accelerating with no one in charge to say, "Let us stop for a while and consider and consolidate what we have." By contrast, if we look at the seventeenth century in The Netherlands, the Golden Age of Dutch art (of which I am quite fond as you know) we see that from its start to its end, not much changed in the way people lived or went about their business. Our times are nothing

---

1 V. W. Odajnyck. 1976. 'Jung and Politics' – Harper and Row –p.115

like that. Change is celebrated; change for change's sake, even if we are not sure whether the change is for the better or for worse. At the same time, the change we celebrate destabilizes us and makes us profoundly anxious.

We call our times "modern." We use this term to indicate that they are unlike anything that went before. To us "modern" means that we consider our own times as discontinuous from the long history of humankind leading up to our appearance on the planet. It comes from the root word "modernus" which means "just now." In terms of the narcissism that naturally flows from that "*now*" mindset, we believe ourselves to be outside of history and often, pretentiously, the culmination of everything that went before. To modern people the fulfillment of the promise of progress has become an inescapable religious dogma. We are also somewhat embarrassed when we look around us and see the mess we have made that we now must live in; we are literally stunned.[1] We cling to the belief that we are superior to those who lived before us, though we have a hard time proving our case, other than pointing to technology. The word modern contains a certain self-congratulation. Yes, technology has advanced tremendously but can we claim that as our own? We are just users of something that was invented by relatively few as a practical application of science, nothing we can lay claim to. The cut-off date between modern and pre-modern seems to be shifting with every generation. The younger generation will find their parents' generation if not pre-modern, then at least old-fashioned, by which they merely mean that they feel advanced in comparison.

---

[1] When we seem to see a rise in stupidity all around us, do not forget that the word stupid comes from "Stupere" which in Latin actually means: "to be stunned or amazed"

Being called old-fashioned has become an indictment of sorts, if not 'hate speech'. However, when you read the letters written by young, in fact very young, soldiers to their home folks during America's Civil War (1861-1865), you will be astonished at their literary quality, their beautiful prose, unambiguous language, often infused with an amazing sense of poetry. Call it old-fashioned if you will, I call it powerful and beautiful. Compare it to our social media posts and see what remains of our pride in modern times. Splendid technology is there, but not quality of thought it seems. Forgive my cynicism, but it seems we have more and faster ways to communicate and less and less to say to each other.

It seems we are in some kind of stupor, an awareness of only the "just now" i.e., modern, without much historical context. This leaves us in a state of continual amazement, stunned by developments because we have little awareness of similar things happening before we were born. The speed of change and the volume of information about everything and anything that assails us every day from everywhere, leaves us in a state of semi-consciousness, which of course, results in our being unaware of the stupor we are in. This makes us vulnerable to all manner of mental instability.

While our time is one of amazing technological progress, it is also, strangely enough, a relapse into barbarism, by which we mean an absence of culture and civility. I love how that is presented by the series of Jurassic Park movies based on Michael Crichton's books. In these we see the great bifurcation inherent in what it means to be modern, the primitive embedded in the most advanced. In these movies, it is not only in the story that we see the primitive—in the form of the dinosaur—as it come into conflict with modern times, but it is also in the technology used in the movie to bring it all to life. It required the most sophisticated movie technology ever developed, to recreate the most primitive state of the world, as presented by these savage creatures who roamed the earth millions of years ago. The dinosaurs reigned the earth longer than they have been extinct. Does our fascination with dinosaurs say something about how we ourselves are still terribly primitive amid all our technological progress? Will the primitive conquer the sophisticated version of the world, as some of the final scenes of the movies seem to suggest: a dinosaur roaring on top of a ruined building which was part of the hi-tech Jurassic theme park?

Carl Jung warned us that high power technology in the hands of barbarians like us is a recipe for disaster. Barbarism is an absence or rejection of any underlying cultural and civilizational structure, allowing cruelty and brutality to come to the fore with more and more devastating consequences, again thanks to sophisticated technology. Here too, the barbaric primitive is fixed firmly in sophisticated technology. The two World Wars in the twentieth century left more dead than all the wars in history combined, thanks to the great technological advances. Such is the power of technology. Though scholars bicker over things like what constitutes a war or how to count war victims, the numbers are all too real and beyond comprehension. Technology knows how to kill us more efficiently and effectively than ever before. Marshall McLuhan, one of the visionary commentators on this modern technological revolution, said that on spaceship earth "there are no passengers, only crew." Indeed, as the current caretaker crew of this planet, if we want to make progress, we need to look towards making progress in terms of culture. This is not as easily done as advancing technology. Evolutionarily speaking it requires a widening of consciousness, more than just the development of thought, which is one on which science depends of course. It requires the overall approach of culture builders, and this is where True Artists come in. Deeply human needs evade technological intervention. Culture grows out of real human needs and human nature resists all attempts at externally engineering a new world. The technology-obsessed amongst us cannot connect with that part of being human and seek technology-inspired solutions to the limitations of technology, thus staying solidly within the technological paradigm. The cultural dimension of life emerges from the depths of our humanity that art alone can provide. Culture, the prerogative of the True Artist, is the inspiration for the way we construct our world, its institutions, its rules, and its laws—not the other way round!

Even the word "culture" has become suspect to the neo-barbarians we have become. Yet, what we call culture is really the only redeeming thing for human beings. Culture comes from below and is not decreed from outside or from above. Culture connects us as human beings; without culture, people perish. They may still be alive, they may still construct tall buildings and fast trains, and make movies with mind-boggling special effects, but they are dead. And as we mentioned before, Carl Jung considered that kind of death-in-life the worst fate that could befall a human being. The word culture includes such things as cultivating, making things grow and tending to something to assure its viability. It also is taking care of the roots of our being human. We can get all wrapped up in the struggles of daily life (including the political wars always erupting), and yet forget about the mystery of just being alive. Culture is not a luxury but a vital component of being alive; that which deals with that mystery, a mystery that touches us for example when a loved one dies.

We all have what I call a "black box" inside of us. The black box is the device in every aircraft that registers

CHAPTER TWENTY

everything that has gone on during the flight. It is what they search for if there has been an accident, a crash, to evaluate what may have gone wrong (actually, it is not black but orange to make it more obvious). Our personal black box is a registry of all that has happened in our personal lives, as well as in the life of our parents, our family, and our family history from long before we were born. Beyond that, it also includes the living history of the society and culture we grew up in, and even the record of humanity as a whole. It is all there, and we carry it around within us, mostly hidden and unconscious. We sometimes get a glimpse of what is there during times of high stress, such as a time of war, when it erupts, and things come spilling out. Old allegiances which were thought dead for generations may come spilling out. That is what we usually call tribal impulses. We may get a glimpse of these things as well in our dreams, if we know how to read them. We often are amazed at the unexpected power and vehemence with which that living history from deep within bursts upon us. We may dismiss it as merely a stress reaction, but it is often so much more, the result of something within us, and often something we are not comfortable dealing with. This material may also be part of what we will later in this book will call "the attic of our life." It is the rich storehouse of inspiration for the True Artist to explore.

I have often wondered why there is such an attraction to the far-off places of the world, the untamed, unpopulated wilds of Antarctica, the jungles of the Amazon, the large nature reserves of Africa filled with wild animals, the deserts of Arabia, the Alaskan wilds. Yes, they are beautiful, but are we actually looking for the large unknown continents of our own selves? Arriving in gigantic floating hotels, the cruise ships, we keep a safe distance from the wilds, ensconced in our modern amenities which all stand for our well-defended ego self. We do the same with the wilds within ourselves, we keep them at a safe distance; they scare us by how they belie our self-evaluation as self-controlled rational beings. Vast regions within us lie unexplored in our unconscious, just as much of the world and space around us remains unexplored. We know little of the depths of the oceans where a mysterious and unexplored universe exists, just as we know little of our own selves. We are attracted to images that give expression to that untamed part of our existence. Art, our image-making faculty, connects us with that part and is the source of images. It is the essence of our "unconscious," a term we use for that vast continent of which we are unaware but which is yet a most important part of us. That same image-making faculty is what operates in our dreams; our spontaneously generated home movies where we "see" things in detail while "being in the dark" because we have our eyes closed! Our inner vision instrument, independent from the tools of our waking seeing, produces and directs those wild tales of wonder within us.

Why muse on these things? Because for a True Artist, art is not just about producing interesting, arresting "stuff" but about tending the flame of culture and preventing it from going out. For the True Artist some of that connection comes through our dreams. Our dreams have their own meaning and most intimately connect us with our deeper selves. However, they are like a foreign language to us, and though not ir-rational, they are non-rational. They have their own logic, so when we say that a dream we had "doesn't make sense" it is a misunderstanding, because it *does* make sense, but in a way very different from our rational, awake self. Our dreams are logical—"psycho-logical"—and are the foundations of the True Artist's endeavors.

CHAPTER TWENTY

In our technology driven times we get the idea that dreams are like an overnight re-starting of our inner computer, where the settings are recalibrated, unleashing a flood of images. But if this dismissive view of dreams were true, the images released in our minds would still be interesting in that they differ greatly from one person to the next. Exploring their particular nature will release meaning beyond what we can think up. Great artists of any sort are in touch with those things because for them this connection with meaning become a daily occupation.

The language of the dream[1] is quite different from our daily life experience yet uses imagery that is familiar and common. This is the very definition of poetics. It is strangely familiar but without the imposed coherence of our daily world experience. I am convinced that we dismiss dreams as meaningless because we are afraid of our own uncharted wilderness. The True Artist endeavors to establish a connection with that part of themselves. And in his or her art the True Artist explores the foundations of what it means to be human in this particular time and space.

The discovery of the unconscious makes a big dent in our sense of self-importance. It is on par with realizing that the sun does not revolve around the earth and that we are just one of the planets revolving around the sun. Darwin's assertion that we supposedly come from the apes was another such blow. These discoveries had an enormous impact and led to the modern mindset. Though the unconscious was well known to the ancient wise men and women of India, and that the earth revolved around the sun was known in

---

1   And we would include here spontaneous day "dreams" as well, and unsolicited insights and inspirations. Also see Anthony Stevens book: Private Myths, on the meaning of dreams.

the 4th century BC in ancient Greece, it never took hold in the mind of contemporary people until it was determined to be so by modern science.

At night, with our mind in sleep mode, all this knowledge awakens. Many artists have realized their dreams as inexhaustible sources of creativity. Though our dreams are our own, we must study to understand their message as if they were a foreign language, as if they were from somewhere other than our own psyche. Many great artists and scientists have done so and found their deep inspiration in dreams. Thankfully, many have left records of how they came to understand their dreams. Yet, the dream is a closed book to most, alas. When rightly understood, our dreams have a special power all their own. Understanding our dreams and using them in doing our work is a special art and deserves special attention. (I simply mention this here because it demands another whole work to deal with their impact.) The route that many follow is to go to websites dedicated to dream decoding. Manuals that explain the symbolism of dreams that have been popular since ancient times, but they are not the most productive. They appeal more to our desire to "tame" our dreams into manageable units of understanding and tend to devalue the infinite richness of them. Our fascination by what comes out of our own being yet seems so "other," is often accompanied by a certain anxiety, because we feel we are confronted by the non-rational part of ourselves.

We do not have to become experts in dream analysis, but we can start by no longer dismissing our dreams as meaningless and being open to what they may reveal to us. Most dream experts recommend starting a dream journal as a first step where we simply record our dreams. Or as some of my students did, they recorded their dreams on their phones and then later transcribed them thereby avoiding turning on a light, grabbing a pen and writing, and thus disturbing our sleep. Dreams are fugitive enough as they are and the fewer the impediments to recording them, the better. Sometimes I also like to make a little primitive drawing to remind myself of some part of the dream.

Exploring the "attic treasures" of our memories is also a way to find inspiration from within. The main thing for the True Artist remains to enlist all of who we are in the work we do. Our memories function in that way very well and are more accessible to most of us than our dreams. We are just trying to make a connection with the unconscious part of us, the seat of creativity.

Love is one of the most amazing products of the unconscious. Can we explain love rationally? No! It defies rational explanations, as do our dreams, but it is ever so real. Love is a mixture of the emotional, the sensuous, the erotic, the aesthetic; is there anything more non-rational than love? Love does not make rational sense. Everyone who has had the good fortune of having fallen in love knows that it is a magnificent experience, complete in itself. It is both a totally unique experience and one shared with all others of the human race. When we are in love it feels like we are the first and only ones in history to have ever experienced it. Yet we know rationally that millions and millions of others have experienced it and are experiencing it. Likewise, it is the nature of the unconscious that it is totally unique and yet shared by all humanity. It is as old as time and as common as having a body, yet it remains ever new and exclusive, and elusive. It can only be grasped by poetry. Love poetry has always been popular, through all ages, and in all cultures. Love songs have always been popular and will remain so. People fall in love even in the direst of circumstances.

Love stories are popular worldwide. Some of it makes it into spiritual literature, like Krishna's amorous exploits from thousands of years ago, and inspires the subject of many profound spiritual books, or into the myths of the Greek gods with all their sordid love affairs, both among themselves and with mortals. Some of the greatest literature has been written about love, love longed for, love found, love lost. Some of the greatest art has been made about love. The most committed rationalist longs for love. That non-rational thing called love is an important part of anyone's life. No one has to be taught about love; we all come equipped for it. Because we were made to love and be loved, we either have it or are painfully aware of its absence. This is the most basic language of our vast unconscious and understood by billions of peoples around the world and throughout history. This is really what is meant when a great artist said that art is love made visible.

All this demonstrates that dreams are a powerful tool for artists. They are what some psychologists call "a royal road" to some of our greatest cultural achievements. For us, dreams and dream-like material fit in well with our idea of suggestive hints mentioned in our introduction. They are markers on our destiny's path. Great empires came from dreams, both in Judeo-Christian scriptures as well as Vedic (Hindu) scriptures and Islamic scriptures, dreams lead to world historical consequences.

Reading about the impact of dreams on culture, religion, art, and politics, is a great way to expand the mind! Now all we need is a good search engine to lead us deeper into the subject matter, where before it was often buried in obscure books. I wonder if the present generation realizes that they are the first ones in history to have such a powerful tool at their disposal. Once you start on a search, for example, on

CHAPTER TWENTY

how dreams have impacted history, or art, you immediately find a lot about the science of dreams. However, it takes a much more intensive search to find how the very framework of science itself has been influenced by dreams.

People who take drugs also acknowledge that there is a large inner realm of creativity and wisdom that can be accessed. Why would you take drugs if you did not believe that there was some vast inner realm of creative potential that could be accessed, and which is not immediately available to the day-to-day mind? If it did not exist, what good would drugs do? Anyone who believes that they are more creative when they take drugs or drink alcohol is tacitly admitting that rationality is not the central truth for them. It is hard to argue against the great advances that our reliance on reason have brought. But here, as in other instances we looked at, it is wrong to stretch this truth into areas where it no longer applies. Researchers like Oscar Janniger have written extensively about the use of drugs and creativity. One simple take-away from his research is that even if drugs open certain channels of inspiration, they limit the ability to execute the supposedly "brilliant ideas" that flow from it. Taking drugs or alcohol may open some of the channels to the creative unconscious, or at the least put our inhibitions on hold, but it impairs our ability to act on our insights, and thus comes into direct confrontation with one of the major pillars of the True Artist: mastery.

The True Artist is an artist of Truth, capital "T," meaning that he or she is not aiming at making spectacular displays of art world fireworks (although that may happen) but is engaged in daily confrontation with life on all levels, obvious and hidden, and making art from it, about it. The True Artist sees the foundational—though often hidden—reality in the obvious. That is the defining element of poetry which transcends the immediate, the urgent, the news of the day, and expresses the universal in the immediate. The immediate is always contaminated by the irrelevant. The poetic, linguistic as well as visual, transforms facts into truths and these truths are wider than our rational mind. Poetry connects us to the unconscious storehouse of creativity.

In our contemporary world where the mythologies of many cultures mix and mingle, artists can no longer assume that their audience will know the mythical narrative stories to which artists of other ages could readily refer, knowing their audience would understand the reference. When societies were more cohesive and had their own realm of influence, theirs was a shared understanding of mythic stories, including the stories of religion. The great themes of civilization, the themes which connect us with our origins, the deepest roots of our being, our ancestry, are drowning in a sea of connectivity engulfing the world, which makes us not more but less connected to the source of our humanity. The only hope we have of living and working authentically as True Artists is to connect to that realm of inner vision without eyes. There is where we engage the seat of our humanity and connect with the human race, mostly without our conscious input.

Japanese people may point to Hokusai's famous woodblock image of a giant wave as a typically Japanese iconic image. Yet, while essentially Japanese in character its appeal proves universal. In this lies a great truth. For Dutch people, the great painter Rembrandt has similar characteristics. He is universally admired, and rightfully so. As an aside, it also helps that he was so prolific that almost all great museums of the world can have their own Rembrandt. (Similarly, Hokusai's universality was helped by modern

CHAPTER TWENTY

printing methods and now the internet.) However, to a Dutch eye, Rembrandt is quintessentially Dutch. The thing we are interested in here is that by thoroughly embodying the Dutch spirit, Rembrandt created the portal through which he became universal. The universal is the collective unconscious of the human race as a whole. The Netherlands are but a tiny speck on the world map, but it can plumb its own universal depths. Da Vinci's universality is beyond doubt. Surely the newly discovered Da Vinci work "Salvatore Mundi" which recently sold for almost half a billion (yes, billion!) dollars to a Saudi sheik dispels any doubts about that. He is universally acknowledged, though his work is very much Italian Renaissance in nature. Each of our small, individual lives are similarly portals to the large, universal life, where we connect with all. No need to aim for something universal, simply adjust the Dutch saying I have mentioned before,[1] "Just be yourself, that is plenty universal!"

While scholars may search for tangible connections that explain certain phenomena (like the universality of Van Gogh's work), they are missing the connections that a good depth psychologist can rather easily identify. Scholars are too often married to the rational and search for concrete, tangible cause-and-effect connections, but these things are all part of the non-rational part of our being in the world. The True Artist's work is done by finding the connection with one's own self, and oneself as part of the great underlying collectivity of humanity, that universality which underlies our individuality and resides in the collective unconscious. That is where the "world soul," what depth

---

[1] "Doe maar gewoon dat doe je al gek genoeg" – "Just be normal, that is plenty crazy"

psychologists call the "anima mundi," resides. Perhaps only an invasion of slimy green aliens from a distant planet would shock us into understanding how much we all belong to that one species called humanity.

CHAPTER TWENTY-ONE

A Messy Divine Order

It bears stressing how much the pursuit of mastery is essential in the life of the True Artist. Mastery for the True Artist can be defined as transforming competency into poetics, turning vision into an artist's voice. This transformation is done in the artist's studio. The True Artist speaks directly, meaning that the True Artist is not someone who merely expresses himself, but an artist who has done the work to discover that actual "self" to be expressed. That self is given form in a workshop of some kind, a studio of some sort, a place away from too much scrutiny.

For me the emblematic studio is the one of the Greek god Hephaestus. Let's dig a bit into the mythology around that ancient Greek god because it so beautifully reveals, in narrative form, the archetypal aspects of the True Artist's destiny. Hephaestus, also called Vulcan by the Romans, is the "artist god." His brother and sister gods and goddesses on Mount Olympus, the realm of the gods, seem engaged in an endless soap opera of love intrigues and power games, which strike us as all too human in their silliness. In contrast, Hephaestus is the only god who actually does work, makes things, creates, rather than just luxuriate in being divine. He does this in a metallurgy workshop. This workshop is symbolic of how True Artists come into their own.

Hephaestus workshop-slash-studio is a place hidden in the depths of the earth (in some versions of the myth in the depths of the ocean). Because the art he practices is metallurgy, it is a place of roaring fires in which metal is formed into weaponry, shields, and most exquisite jewelry objects. True Artists, as kids, start out in like manner in somewhat hidden fashion. This is where they come into their own while growing up amidst all the family goings on.

His workshop must be seen as an allegorical representation of the artist studio. Other parts of the story can be understood as well as aspects of the psychological make-up of the True Artist. His divine and dysfunctional family is uncomfortable with his presence. His own mother Hera, wife of Zeus, is the one who casts him out. Disappointed that he is not a beautiful physical specimen like his brother Ares (Mars), the god of war, who has the good looks and a muscular build that make her proud, she sees Hephaestus more as a personal failure. He has some deformities that make him undesirable as her son; she is after all a goddess. She literally throws him out of the house and down the mountain. Tumbling down from the divine heights of Mount Olympus he rolls deep into the earth or the ocean. Away from the family, rejected, away from the realm of the gods, even though a god himself, he sets up shop beneath the earth. This is very much like the True Artist who usually and quite organically sets up shop in elementary ways somewhere in the environment they grow up in, in a somewhat hidden fashion, away from prying eyes. Thus they start doing what they are quite naturally meant to do—they start carving their path of destiny.

The story of Hephaestus throws a light on many aspects of the True Artist's life. It is not uncommon that young True Artists face rejection from their family because the father or mother had envisioned a different kind of offspring, or because their siblings are uncomfortable with their approach to life. I have shared about how that unfolded in my own life. It seems to come with the territory. If lucky, the aspiring artist is supported, but it is not the norm. I have taught students whose parents were artists themselves and it does seem to give "a leg up," though that too is uncertain; however most seem to be refugees from families that were not fully understanding.

The way Hephaestus is finally brought back to the family is a story rich with psychological meaning, which can serve as another one of our "suggestive hints." At some point Hephaestus creates a brilliant golden throne for his mother, the one who rejected him, which he then sends up to Mount Olympus. Once there, his mother tries out this brilliantly crafted throne and the brilliance of the workmanship becomes evident in several ways. After his mother Hera sits down, invisible clasps come down on her, and she is stuck on the throne. It seems Hephaestus is getting back at his mother for rejecting him. This is not an uncommon story in life either, but Hephaestus does it through his mastery! It is a negative way of using mastery, something to be avoided by regular humans, for it destroys whatever is good about the artistic endeavor. Still, it is ever so effective and serves in this story to show the power of superlative craftsmanship. Unable to get off the throne, his enraged mother sends her favorite son, Ares, to get his brother from the bowels of the earth to free her from the throne. But Hephaestus does not cooperate and Ares' mission fails. It seems Hephaestus is full of anger at his mother, and who can blame him? Eventually it is his half-brother Dionysus, also known as Bacchus the god of ecstasy (and not, as commonly assumed, the god of drunkenness), who gets him to come home to free mom. For this Dionysus first gets him inebriatred to then mount him on a donkey to take him home to Mount Olympus. After freeing mom from her throne, Hephaestus is now recognized by his brothers and sisters for his superb abilities, and requests for jewelry, weaponry and special accoutrements come his way. This too is emblematic of many a young True Artist's life. Often, he or she has been developing special skills in privacy, in his or her "hidden place" away from the gaze of others. These special skills, through some special circumstances, are then brought out in the open, brought to the surface so to speak, and get recognition for their special character. In the mythological story, Hephaestus then becomes recognized as special by those who have before rejected him. Part of this is recognition is getting the prize of marriage to the goddess of sensual love Aphrodite (Venus). But if you think that is the end of his troubles, it is not. Eventually she will cheat on him with his brother Ares, and the rest of the family will again turn on him for being such a fool to be cheated on.

Mythological narrative is often superior to a lot of modern psychological pseudo-scientific lingo, though the form of a narrative requires some imaginative thinking and work to understand. For me the narrative of Hephaestus speaks of the True Artist in the making. He or she starts like Hephaestus, quite naturally fashioning some sort of workshop, some kind of creative space. This is an early version of what will later develop into a full-fledged studio, atelier, or creative working space, literally or figuratively. Some will eventually build a great and perfect studio, while others prefer a less developed raw space, still others create a space in a corner of the home. This space is present in some rudimentary form in all True Artists' lives. Look for it, and you will find it. This space is part of your being.

CHAPTER TWENTY-ONE

A rather dramatic and theatrical example of this feature of the True Artist is the painter, Francis Bacon. One of the great modern artists, he almost became fused with his creative space. Throughout his career he remained in the same small, simple, low-rent studio where he had started out. He remained there after his career had taken off and made him a millionaire. It was a messy, uncouth workshop with piles of empty paint tubes from many years of painting (I know this from someone who visited him in his studio), and in it he fashioned works of art that look cleanly done when displayed on the pristine walls of museums or galleries. Bacon seemed to have worked best in that kind of cluttered, messy environment. It is where he went "underground." He dismissed those who called the clutter and disarray a "mess," and proclaimed it instead a "divine order." It is interesting that he would call it divine, since the Hephaestus underground studio was divine as well. I am sure he meant it to refer to a higher order of things, which may look messy to the common eye. He saw order where others saw disorder and he needed it just that way to do his work. He accepted that part of himself as essential while others considered it uncouth. He knew it as the fertile ground of his creativity. The life that seems merely disorderly to others, may be the divine order of a True Artist. For me personally, a neat and organized studio is not conducive to work, while too much disorder likewise makes it hard to work. Cleaning up a messy studio is something that I put off until I can put it off no longer! But in no time flat, the same orderly disorder reappears.

Years ago, I read an article about then world chess champion, Bobby Fisher, which made it clear that his apartment was a messy affair, with laundry and stuff lying all around. However, at its center stood a pristine, well-organized chessboard, like an altar, where it seems he ordered his world as Bacon did at his easel. It is a higher order or perhaps a deeper order. That Hephaestus has his studio-workshop underground is telling, and archetypal because for the depth psychologist it means we are in the realm of the unconscious.

A very telling, but somewhat strange acknowledgement that the creative space is very much part of a True Artist's life is that Bacon's studio, in all its messiness, was recreated as part of the museum in Dublin, Ireland. The experts, always attracted to the dramatic aspects of an artist's life, saw it as part of his creative output and believed it afforded a glimpse into the inner workings of his genius. In their estimation, the man, the work, and the working space, all blended together to produce his art. Bacon's example is somewhat extreme and dramatic, but very much illustrative of the reality of the True Artist's life.

I have known several people who with much effort and forethought built their perfect studio and then, when it was all done, moved! When the studio was "just right" they sold their house and went elsewhere! How strange is that, I thought, when I saw the same pattern followed by different people; now I understand better what it may have been about. It is an acknowledgement of the importance of that creative space, but a misinterpretation of what the space is all about. It is about creating an environment for creation. For one artist friend, it was because she felt her beautifully equipped and built-up studio did not inspire her, and she needed a more basic, organic type of life. She moved to a small town (with a rich history) in Italy, set up shop there and was quite successful. With another, I believe it was because his talent was more that of an architect, a technical person, which was his real art, though he produced

CHAPTER TWENTY-ONE

paintings as well, which were rather schematic and architectural in nature. He was proficient in design and may not have moved past that proficiency to mastery. For technique to be turned into mastery some need a messy studio or move to a small village in Italy, while for others the journey is an inward experience.

CHAPTER TWENTY-TWO
Genius and Mastery

Since we know that mastery comes from proficiency made larger, we are confronted with the question, what proficiency should we pursue? What skill is called for? Ultimately almost any expertise can set you on the path to mastery, but it is always best to choose to concentrate in an area where you have a natural inclination. When considering art most people's thinking turns towards drawing, painting, or sculpting; or better to making paintings and making sculpture or with music, playing a certain instrument. There are many ways to approach that important question of one's area of proficiency. If wood working is your thing, then make that your path to mastery. The focus of this book is the creative arts, those creative acts that address the soul of society and of the individual, whatever they might be.

It is quite a common attribute of the True Artist to have several areas of interest, thus choosing can be a challenge. I remember when facing that dilemma myself I happen to read the brilliant biography on Honoré de Balzac by the talented Stephan Zweig. Balzac is certainly one of the greatest writers France every produced and that is saying a lot because the French produced a lot of great writers. Balzac's work ethic and discipline, as I read about them in Zweig's book, were rather scary to me at the time because I could not

CHAPTER TWENTY-TWO

see myself able to muster that kind of dedication. I remember feeling disturbed about the obsessive character so well described in the biography. Balzac developed an unequaled mastery of language. It is a great exposé of the True Artist life, in all its glory and its pain. As already noted, he too, was not sure whether he should be a painter or a writer. He started out as a commercial writer and later complained that he could never completely rid himself of the commercial "tricks" he learned being a commercial artist. This is another aspect that will speak to a lot of us. I personally am grateful for the "tips" and "tricks" I picked up from doing commercial work, though I am aware of the challenges they pose in going beyond them.

Many True Artists have questions like: music or visual art? Some practice all, but almost always focus on one being the core of their mastery. Leonardo da Vinci is reported to have been a superb musician (who even taught others to play an instrument) and was a maker of instruments as well. He exemplified many things that sparked the notion of a "Renaissance man," which we call someone who is proficient in different creative fields. He had a contentious relationship with painting, falling in and out of love with it, while pursuing his many other interests. These interests led to scientific conclusions which have only been corroborated as recently as a few years ago by scientists. From how I read it, he pursued painting in the same way he pursued his scientific interests, because painting at that time was being "discovered" and what we now take for granted had not yet become common knowledge. His mastery was that of an inquisitive mind that spread out over many different disciplines. We must be careful with a true genius like Da Vinci because genius is exactly that which defies definition and cannot easily be understood, if at all. Looking at a life like his life we may get a wrong sense of permission, that somehow, we do not have to make up our minds about a definite core expertise to follow. Genius is as genius does. It is very rare.

RIGHT CHOICE, WRONG REASON

Although I was not quite aware of the relationship of skill to mastery when choosing what skills to acquire in depth, I chose painting. Happily, I chose right, but I did so for the wrong reason. It did not really make a difference looking back, but it is important to achieve some clarity on it. I was under some pressure because at that point I had that dreaded realization that my life was not working, that something was off. With my two academic degrees, I stood lost in the world. This is a rather common experience, where we spent a lot of years becoming proficient in something that we then abandon. This is no big thing, if you can see the expertise gained as a first step on the road to mastery even in a different kind.

The awareness that I should change course came from a sense of misery. "Misery leads to mastery," my mentor told me. Well, that may be so, but it can also lead to giving up. Yes, the road to mastery knows its miseries. My own personal misery finally opened my eyes. I knew that something was askew, if not with me, then with the life I was living. That is when I started to reorient myself towards art. Why? Because that is what I had always been pursuing naturally, as a kid, as a young man, as a grown man. I had always carved out some kind of working space, no matter how minimal, to do "my work," even though I would not have been able to name it at the time. I always felt that I understood art at a deeper level than others and had a natural feel for the materials and the process of art making. Strangely enough, but painfully revealing of my psychological make up, just because I had that natural feel for it, I dismissed it as inconsequential and unimportant. Living had to be a challenge for it to be real, or so I thought! I had not yet remembered that episode I related earlier when my high school teacher had shamed me into realizing that I must write "cogent" essays, rather than "lyrical" ones, because lyricism was not something that would get you places. I had also forgotten my immediate and natural contrarian response, never spoken but ever reverberating in my mind, "I can do that at *any* time!" A stronger personality would have taken that as a sign that I knew what I knew and that an unhappy teacher should not dissuade me. Alas, that was not the kind of kid I was. I did not have that spirited sense of self! With hindsight and from the point of view of my training I can point to some psychological crossroads where the damage to my sense of self was done, but it resulted in a certain kind of inner shut down, that now I had to deal with. Done right, it strengthens you in the end. As a kid I had been ebullient and full of energy with an unrelenting creative go-for-it spark. This exhausted the adults around me and they gave me the message that I should somehow tone it down. Later, my memory of that sparky kid I was, has remained a sign that it was in me after all and could be retrieved somehow.

THE LOWEST COMMON DENOMINATOR

In the context of this book, reorienting my life towards art may look like a positive breakthrough, but it felt more like a defeat! It is best described by the words that spontaneously came to mind once I finally decided. This is how it presented itself. I felt that I had come all the way down to my "lowest common denominator." Those exact words arose in my mind and did not make sense to me at that time. Though "encrypted," the message was very clear, and once "decoded" turned out to be spot on. I did not understand it then, but that did not diminish the power of the communiqué from within. "Lowest common denominator," what a strange way to think about it! Yet I could not get rid of that insight. Though I rationally dismissed it and tried to rephrase it, it remained insistent within my mind. It was something from deep within or from higher up; either way, I could not escape the grip this formulation had on me, and that is why I remembered it over all these years. Though it seemed nonsensical, it turned out to be nonsensical in the way dreams are nonsensical from a logical point of view, yet having a deeper meaning. How right I was to call it that! It may have been because I was stuck in feelings of failure at the time and could not see the truth of it.

The truth was and is, that art making has always been the "lowest common denominator" in all I have done in life. The stance of the artist was how I approached life at every stage, in every circumstance, whether I was already making work or not. It is the True Artist's stance. Life did not make sense to me unless I gave it form in some way; it is how my being works. Not doing it leaves a gnawing absence within, and not identifying that absence for what it is can make you quite miserable. Everything is grist for the creative mill of the True Artist, whether messy or orderly. Underneath all the outward occurrences and happenings was the steady stream of making art out of it all, even if it took years, a lifetime! It was "low" in the sense of what the alchemists call the "prima materia." This is a term used by them to designate the crude base materials, which they aim to transmute into gold. For me this has meant that the occurrences of life,

CHAPTER TWENTY-TWO

the simple things that make up our daily life, were the base material from which I attempted to make gold: something *meaningful*. It was the urge, not just to create, not just to express myself, but to live out my destiny as a True Artist. In what way do you, dear reader and compatriot, see yourself doing that? You would not be reading this unless you have that basic reality within you too.

Paints and brushes, pencils and pens, these are all very basic, time-tested utensils, and they have always been natural tools for me. At the time of deciding, I felt, and rightly so, that I had descended to that very basic reality which I had already known before I got all sophisticated and cultured in the university. Undeniably it was something that I naturally understood; simple, yes, basic, yes, but real and tangible. We see the same principle operating when we talk about finding the genius part within. I had built up this whole intellectual persona, one that was way too sophisticated for my own good, or to do such "lowly work" as using pencil or brush (I feel sad and worried that computer programs have taken the pencil and brush out of the hands of so many aspiring True Artists). It would become a major challenge to bring up my skills to the level of my intellectual prowess, such as it was. When studying philosophy with another wonderful mentor, we were discussing art and artists from the philosopher's point of view and during one of those conversations I had this startling realization—I am not here to talk about it, I am here to *do* it! Of course, there is no way to take thinking out of the art making process. We need it, but thinking tends to take over and before you know it, you are more of an art critic than an art maker. You are in danger of becoming a cultural critic when your thinking exceeds your ability to *do*. Of course, thinking is an art in itself, and is certainly part of making art, but thinking tends to easily take over and dominate. It was Peter Paul Rubens who acknowledged that fact at the end of the 16th century. He is the great and enormously successful painter (in his own times) from Antwerp, now in Belgium, working a generation before Rembrandt in the Netherlands. He realized that painters needed to be distinguished from craftsmen (whom they were lumped in with in the guilds), exactly because they brought vision and thought to craft and skill, and therefore needed their own guild. He gave them the name of "Pictor doctus," the "thinking artist," to distinguish them from the crafts people. And the modernist shift to conceptual art is part of that dictatorship of thought taking over. We see the same in modern architecture.

For me it was a real struggle to satisfy that "smart aleck" part of me, that irritating part that believed it already knew everything somehow. Yes, it was knowledgeable, but out of alignment with the rest of me, the doing part of me. How do you deal with that? Eventually I found an analogy that exposed for me the heart of the matter. It was in the mysterious metamorphosis of the silkworm that I found a favorite analogy, a metaphor for the True Artist's struggle. At a certain point the silkworm, a rather elementary crawling creature, "knows" that "it's time!" and starts spinning a cocoon around itself. Having completed the cocoon around itself. the silkworm starts to dissolve most mysteriously into a gooey, dark, undifferentiated mass. Yet, within that undifferentiated mass there remains some central intelligence at work. There is a knowing operating there that understands how to transform itself from gooey mass into a delicate moth-butterfly creature with gossamer wings. A most miraculous transformation! That transformation is just one of the many that exists on our planet. It seems the silk moth-butterfly is the true destiny of the erstwhile worm, thus going from earthbound, crawling creature, to being able to fly! It is a magical development which is more than going from here to there; it is profound, it is transformation, the fulfillment of a destiny. There can be no butterfly creature without the worm first crawling on the earth. Such it seems to be with the True Artist destiny. Even the silk that is harvested from its cocoon, one of the world's most highly prized materials, is to me a proper metaphor for the way of the True Artist's path. One could stop at the cocoon stage and spin its silkiness into a beautiful career, but then you will be stopped by the silk merchants of the world on your way to fulfilling your True Artist destiny. The metaphor works on many levels.

CHAPTER TWENTY-THREE
Follow Your Passion

Passion is a subject which demands to be dealt with. When I hear people advising others "to follow their passion," I am of two minds about it; I agree, and I disagree. Passion can be short-lived as in sexual passion, a flame that burns bright and then spends itself quickly. This is how most of us understand passion. You can have a passion for music, but that too may be a quick burn type passion. You may have a passion for painting, but do you have the kind of passion that it takes to live the *life* of an artist, a True Artist, always "on" never "off"? That is another matter altogether. I never want to put cold water on someone's fiery passion, but sometimes a bit of cold water to bring down the temperature and convert it into a steady, yet intense flame, a "smolder," is exactly what is needed. My substitute grandmother's remark, "Aren't you reaching too high?" can be seen as such a water dousing. What she could have said, and what I needed to hear, (which she was incapable of saying) was, "How steady is your passion? How hard are you willing to work to give it the depth that you feel in your passion for it?" Coming from a generation that had gone through the horrors of war, passion was not exactly something they could relate to. For most people during the war years, the years of oppression, the most common thought was to just get back to 'normal life'. A life of passion was not anything they were aiming at. When a passion is true, it means that it belongs to the essence of a person, it cannot be snuffed out, cannot be extinguished; so, a water dousing is no catastrophe.

When my substitute grandmother said that I might be aiming 'too high', she seemed to presume that the artist's life is somehow 'high', a loftier way of being. It is not. The True Artist is a part of the life of the community in a most common and most necessary way. In terms of culture, those who bind people on a very basic level, we can call them "essential workers," and like all essential workers, their task is basic. Their passion is a solidly based one.

Passions are not the same as desires. I may desire to be an artist, but when I have a passion for it, it arises from a different place within, a place beyond my control. We use the word passion, because we want to indicate that it is not a rational decision. Desires are not rational either of course, but by calling it a passion, we mean that it has deeper roots. Surprisingly, the root of the word passion is "pati" which means to suffer! It is used that way when they speak of "the passion of the Christ;" it talks about suffering!

When we call someone a genius, we often mean to indicate that their passion has roots, not just in the specific personality of the person, but in the larger collective destiny, the collective unconscious, which genius somehow has access to. The unconscious is not some kind of storage space but a living, moving psychic realm. It is comprised of both negative stuff that we have repressed, as well as positive potential, waiting to be realized. When we say that someone "has their finger on the pulse of the time," we are referring to a person having a special connection with the instinctive knowing of the collective, that which we indicate with the term "unconscious." The genius people themselves may not even be aware of having such a connection, they just act from it. If indeed they are not aware of it, they may all at once find themselves disconnected from it and wonder what happened and may have no idea how to reconnect. I am using the word passion here for a deep, smoldering enthusiasm, an enthusiasm which though waxing and waning as the tides of the ocean, remains constant. Passion harnessed to serve the artist's vision is what the True Artist is about. Our individual creative imagination is "on loan" from the collective unconscious imagination; therefore to claim it as exclusively one's own puts an unnecessary strain on creativity. Though involving hard work, creativity is "received" rather than pursued; the hard work *is* the receiving.

To get to know the True Artist within is not just some ego-preoccupation. Just as there is consciousness in that black mass of the silkworm within its cocoon, the undifferentiated form of us has within it, the consciousness of the True Artist. The black mass turns into a finely winged creature; giving shape to our destiny is our work.

You can also beautifully visualize this consciousness from the perspective of a hologram, and call it a holographic kernel. A technological marvel, a hologram shows us a 3-dimensional world, but it is unsubstantial, made up of light alone. The kernel of truth within you which knows what it is supposed to be, is likewise still unsubstantial, like the hologram. While the hologram is made up of light waves, the hologram inside of you is made up of psychic waves. It is quite fully there. And, like the most amazing aspect of a hologram that fits our situation as well, if you cut up the hologram, within each part so cut up, the full image of the whole is present. Such is the reality of True Artists, whether in the beginning phases of the path or well on their way.

CHAPTER TWENTY-THREE

We have intelligence operating in us long before we become conscious of it, long before our awareness has started to dawn. It is there from the start. The True Artist path especially is about discovering the true intent inherent in our being. There is a consciousness within that leads us on, even if it confuses us or makes us unhappy or depresses us. We learn to discern it amid all the contradictions; the full image is already present in all its cut-up parts.

When we say we are depressed, we are saying that something is being pressed down, de-pressed. Contrary to how we talk about depression, it is an active thing. It is the action of suppressing something within which demands to be recognized. It takes a lot of energy to do so. This is why I suggested that we supplant saying, "I am depressed" with "I am de-pressing something," which would give some immediate clarity to the situation.[1]

Many of us, struggling to embrace the True Artist within, are often told things when we are young: "well, you sure have a vivid imagination," or "do you always imagine things, rather than see what is there?" This is meant to shut us up, because the not-so-imaginative types do not like to be shown up as being unimaginative. This seems to be a very basic division in humanity. "Imagination rules the world," Napoleon proclaimed. Being above all a man of vision, he knew all too well that his strategic prowess was just his proficiency, but that his imaginative vision was his mastery.

Imagination is being able to see beyond what is directly available, the obvious. It often threatens the people we grow up with unless we are lucky and grow up with imaginative people, or those who make a place for what we bring. I now

---

[1] Psychologists however also acknowledge that there is such a thing as 'clinical depression' which is something that requires proper treatment.

can see clearly how close I sometimes came to accepting the verdict that I had "too much imagination." It is true that you can get lost in fantasy, which is often mistaken for imagination. Imagination is a great gift. At some point the person of imagination realizes that it is also a burden, because of other people's instinctive discomfort with those with imagination. We must get used to that. And we must also remember to keep our imagination in proper proportion, because it is nothing but an ability you were blessed with, and not some private property. It is a great tool, like any talent you have. It was *given* to you, a gift. One of the ancient Vedic scriptures, the Srimad Bhagavatam, older than any of our Bibles, says, "You have been born into this world for the benefit of mankind. And yet, you allow emotions to delude you. Remember who you are!"

CHAPTER TWENTY-FOUR
The Attic of Our Life

One way of discovering who you are, is to rummage through what I like to call "our attic," something which I have alluded to in several places already. It is a personal "psychic attic"–filled with memories and reminiscences, gathering dust and rust. But what we keep there can help us identify the path of our True Artist destiny, in our own life and times. This attic is an archetypal presence. The attic has a special place in stories, fairy tales, and movies, and is, in one guise or another, a theme in all our lives. It is the place where things that we think have outlived their usefulness, but we are not quite prepared to throw out yet, end up. We store things there that we, or generations before us, deemed to still have some value, some potential that we did not quite see at the time, but felt. We intuited that there may come a time when these things might become valuable to us again. Not many houses have attics these days. The function of the attic has now been usurped by garages that are filled to the brim, leaving no space for the cars for which they are intended. More ominously, there are now the self-storage places that have sprung up all around where the hidden history of the country is chattering away. While the attic is part of our home, part of us really, the storage place is separate and more disconnected from us. But archetypally they seem to serve the same purpose, though less romantically so.

The fabled and somewhat mythical concept of the attic remains psychologically significant. As kids we may go on a treasure hunt in the attic where we find the remains of lives from the past and somehow feel an organic connection with them. It is a place of mystery, a bit foreboding, a bit scary. Kids love to rummage through scary stuff though. They feel a special connection with those unruly mysterious things that we all eventually learn to tame, press down, as we grow. The dread of things gone silent in the attic is like the drumroll in the circus to get our attention to a death-defying stunt. We are intrigued, but there is also a happy aspect to it; a new potential we may discover in things discarded.

Things have often been brought to the attic to be forgotten, but not merely thoughtlessly thrown away. There are also things there that *are* and remain significant in a rarefied kind of way and to be visited only on special occasions. The woman who has her first love letters there in a box may muster the courage to open it and feel those feelings again, to be reconnected with the first luxuriant stirrings of love before 'life took over'. The man who finds his first train set, revisits his first attempts at creating a model of something. Treasured dolls with which we were once intimately connected, tend to end up there; the intense connection we had with them cannot be severed just like that. They are not thrown away, they are "stored" in the attic. When we go there and visit these relics of our past, we fall into a reverie and feelings flood over us. A nostalgic longing may capture us; we may feel a sense of regret, a sense of loss, a sense of the passing of time. We may reconnect with a passion that has somehow gotten lost in the pursuits of our daily lives. In that way we start to understand the times we are living in.

CHAPTER TWENTY-FOUR

There are television programs that hook into that remarkable attic phenomenon. People bring old stuff that they have had in the family for years or generations, to experts to evaluate and appraise. We get pleasure from watching people bring something they are not sure has value, yet has value to them, then learn that it is worth a lot of money. It may be a pillow they have had on the couch for a long time, a rug that no longer fits the new decor, or an intriguing but strange or somewhat decrepit looking box that came in their possession from some distant aunt. Then they discover that it is a collector's item and very valuable. Money is the measurement of its worth, but what about the owners, do they find it worthwhile? We love to see the look on the faces of the man who finds out that that strange looking box in which his mother just kept her rubber bands and paper clips, is a historical treasure, with a long pedigree of use by royals. All at once that box is looked upon with very different eyes; it gains in gravity. If the owner does not immediately run to the nearest auction house, that box becomes an object of power, a significant presence in the house, and a nucleus of special energy. It is now shown off with pride to visitors and looked upon with awe and affection by the owner, as a treasure, a sacred kind of presence, speaking of the importance of their own life. It has become a relic. The writer Iris Murdoch says about relics that they gain their own power even if they are not authentic. By the very fact that they are revered, a power adheres to them. Here we connect this with our psychic storehouse of memories.

The same as in an actual attic we rummage through the psychic attic of our life and find treasures which, almost discarded, show to give meaning to our life. This is very much part of the path of the True Artist and gives form to our destiny. We visit the attic of our life and find things there that we have discarded in our rush to get on with life but which are still emotionally alive. When we take the time for contemplation in the attic, we are almost shocked by how important certain things are in the overall scheme of our lives. In that way, the formula "lowest common denominator" lay in my private psychic attic for a long time before I fished it out from in between all the other memories and realized the significance it carried for me. I was glad I had not discarded it.

Unlike the attic of a house, we carry our own attic with us at all times and can visit it as we wish. Great artists rummage through the attics of their lives and find treasures there that do not need an antique expert to evaluate them but wield their proper value in how they make them part of their artistic output. They accrue value by virtue of their very discovery. They are important to the artist, as well as to those who appreciate the art. Many great artist's piece of scrap paper has been auctioned off for amazing prices, even though you could get a great piece of art by a lesser-known artist for much less. They are treasured for their relic value and as investment rather than for the art. Do not dismiss the concept of relics as something that does not belong in our modern times!

I remember when the Beatles visited Amsterdam at the height of "Beatlemania." The power of their special kind of fame plugged right into something in the spirit of the times and cannot be understood from watching video footage of that time. It was madness, a mania, a kind of hysteria, but also a significant aspect of the spirit of the time. The hotel the Fab Four stayed at auctioned off some of the plates and cups from which they had drunk or eaten during their stay there (or so it was said). Those too became relics, objects to

CHAPTER TWENTY-FOUR

which clung significances that we can barely understand. Relics come in many forms, not just as the bones of saints.

When I came to the National Gallery of Art in Washington, D.C., in 1995 for a history-making special exhibit of more of Vermeer's paintings than had been brought together in that first exhibit in my home town The Hague, I was not surprised to find a line of people stretching around several blocks waiting to get in. Since when, I thought, had Vermeer become so popular? (A recent even larger exhibit of his work in 2023 in Amsterdam, attracted millions of viewers!). But when I started talking to some of the people standing in line, I realized they were all waiting for something very different. They had come to see the display of clothes worn by "Jackie O," the widow of President John F. Kennedy who, after his assassination, married the Greek shipping magnate Onassis. I was happy not to have to stand in that line. It was clear that I could just walk into the Vermeer exhibit without any problem while Jackie O's dresses, modern day relics, had such a spell-binding power all their own that it was worth the wait for so many. I doubt all these people would have come out to see these no doubt worthy creations had they not been worn by an iconic woman like Jackie O.

It does not matter what it is, it matters what meaning we attach to it. This is why you see included in this book many small, apparently insignificant personal memories retrieved from my attic which showed why they had been stored there at all. They found their meaning later as a part of the period I had lived through and what they revealed about my destiny. I believe that we can approach all the aspects of our life that way. The experiences of my life, wrapped up in sketches in the many sketchbooks I have kept over the years and that survived many moves, the myriad notes in many little notebooks, train tickets from travel, concert tickets, they are all my attic treasures. I rummage through them, pull out one or more, examine them and see what unexpected value they may have. I also know that I will never get to all of it.

Oscar Janiger, whose work on creativity and drugs I mentioned before, recently came back into my life because of some sketches I did of him when I attended one of his lectures a long time ago. I had totally forgotten about him and the lecture. I felt that there was a reason why I happened to open that little sketchbook after so many years and landed upon those sketches. These sketches were lying around in my personal attic. After finding them I bought a book about the research he was famous for, which was into the effects of psychedelic drugs on creativity. It was that book that suggested to me to view artists as tending "the flame of culture," which I adopted from his calling artists "keepers of the Promethean flame."[1] I take these chance discoveries seriously and follow them out. To me they are like messages from the I-Ching or some other divinatory procedure. Quite the same as how people opening the Bible randomly, consider the passage they light upon as the appropriate message for that day. Their significance may not be immediately clear, but I am willing to wait and see what develops; I am willing to do some work around it. We all have these "remains," the things that linger in our lives, the attic treasures that are seemingly without value but hold the promise of things to be discovered. We must acknowledge that once we cared enough to collect or create them, and that we have hung onto them. At some level of consciousness, we must have sensed them to have value. Most memories are lost to

---

[1] Marlene Dobkin de Rios, Ph.D. and Oscar Janniger, M.D. 2003. LSD-Spirituality and the Creative Process. Park Street Press. Rochester, Vermont

us, and it is only the ones that are significant in some way that end up in the attic.

When we were preparing to move to a new home, friends advised us to purge and use the move to finally get rid of "all the old stuff." I felt a definite resistance to it, and I wondered if I was merely stubborn and hanging on to things, things that would only weigh me down. Was I too lazy to go through and discard them? But then I realized that things are not the same for me as they are for these well-meaning friends. First, the word "purge" turns me off because it calls forth the idea of someone being hounded out of the party, like Stalin did, holding "purges." It also means to vomit, which certainly does not feel right to me either. Secondly, I instinctively knew that in all that stuff, even that stuff kept in storage for way too long and at too great an expense, there was something of value. Carl Jung was right when he indicated that it is not about living long but living meaningfully. How do you do that? True Artists often do it by going through the remains of their lives and finding in them the deeper meaning we long for. So many things are passed over in the rush of life. They are our own private relics, objects of power that may become a spark to lead us on, or we may find, have led us on all along. We do not need antique experts to convince us of the worth of the things that have lingered in our lives. We are our own expert here; that is what humanizes us, because they are ours alone and cannot be replaced. No one is an expert on my life other than me, not even a good therapist or priest or rabbi. They may be helpers, but I am the ultimate authority. It is the process of becoming an expert on one's own life and then a master of it that is the True Artist's task. It is not egomaniacal self-obsession, but the work of discovering the meaning of life through the only connection we have with life—our own lives. From this we create.

The art literati, the curators, the critics, push it as far as trying to divine from the chaos and clutter of Francis Bacon's studio an insight into his creative process, and even making it into a museum exhibit. The stuff in our psychic attic space is our very own, though not quite a museum exhibit, but also not clutter, rather the psychically alive pieces of our life that are goading us to force them to reveal their meaning.

CHAPTER TWENTY-FIVE
My Father's Piano

Here is one of the treasures I found in the attic of my mind that clarified my destiny. It was all dusty and in need of a polish, but the polish would reveal an important early marker of my lief's path. I want to share with you how that mere "memory-in-the-attic" became a significant signpost. According to my dictionary, a signpost is "something that acts as guidance or a clue to an unclear or complicated issue." For much of my life, it had been mostly just a humorous childhood memory, one that would pop into my mind from time to time, for example, when talking to my brother about growing up together. It was not forgotten, but it was not quite a treasure; for that I needed to do some work and introspection. An attic treasure is a regular memory, something you merely recall, but that reveals itself in a surprising and more expansive manner once "dusted off," which means after you have given it some loving attention. You would not remember it if it did not have some significance, for there are many things that happen to us in our march through life that never attain the status of a memory. Our minds would be overloaded. So, the fact that it is a memory unit at all is an indication of its significance. It is up to us to do something with it. You can do that through giving it form, writing about it, meditating on it, reading about how others have dealt with similar memories, and in general connecting it with things you have found expressed elsewhere, like in movies. Then it gains a larger dimension other than just the cute kind of youth memory it was before. This attic treasure was about my father's piano. And, of course, the whole story around it.

One morning after many years of neglect, it popped into my mind while I was working on a creative project. Rather than dismissing it as, "oh, there is that memory again," I wondered why it would come up at that time. I "saw," rather than just "remembered" that old upright piano. It was somewhat beaten up and had stood in a corner of the simple home—a ground floor really—we lived in for the first six years of my life. I also saw the six-year-old me throwing a major temper tantrum. That was a surprise. This was a part of the memory that I had not really connected with before. That tantrum became an important aspect of it all for me.

I remembered scenes of standing next to that piano with my brother when my mother was playing it, singing maybe Christmas songs, or especially songs dedicated to St. Nicolas. (St. Nicolas is the Dutch version of Father Christmas, or rather the latter is modeled on the former. This is how that guy in the red suit got the name "Ol' Saint Nick.") Ruminating on that I began to see in this domestic scene, stored in the attic of my mind, an early unfolding of my True Artist destiny. You can compare those dusted-off memories with documentaries of "olden times," which are all over the internet. Those that were in black and white are now in color. That added color, a gift from new technology, stands for the way we bring out the significance of our attic memories, we give them back their color. Giving it color, through new technology, is really an attempt to make it all more accessible and give it new meaning. A simple memory

CHAPTER TWENTY-FIVE

is packed with layers of meaning and unpacking them is one of those truly life changing things you can do. For the True Artist, who does not usually get enough guidance, they can be the important self-affirmations that are so hard to get from others. The True Artist whose sense of self identity is strong enough to do without is the exception, not the rule.

The scene unfolds when we were about to move to a new neighborhood. Seemingly unrelated material surfaced in relation to it, and I spun out the story according to what I knew. Our move had to do with my father being able to build up his own business after the total ruination of the war years which had left them with literally nothing at all. Though he was a born entrepreneur, I always suspected that my father's grandest dream had been to be a concert pianist. Not that I think he really had it in him to bring that to a successful outcome, but I deeply suspected that his heart's desire was that, becoming like one of the musicians he so admired. If I could talk to him now and say to him what I just wrote down so many years after his passing, he would dismiss it all and say something kindly like, "oh, those were just youthful dreams, I never was that good." Or if he were in a different mood, he might get irritated with me for bringing it up at all, which is the sign of digging into a memory that hurts. Still, I feel quite convinced of it, and even more so, I believe that the six years old kid I was had an intuitive grasp of the situation. Kids know more than we think, or they can express. Our youthful knowing too often lies scattered about in the attic of our life as so many old letters, smudged, torn, and as yellowed fragments. If we could read these scraps of memory paper, they would put us back in touch with the passionate spaces we once inhabited. The glow of our wonderful insights and dreams would overwhelm us and leave us wondering about the magic depth of feeling we had then. I believe I had a sense of my father's dreams.

My father did not exactly have an easy time as a youth in a Germany where the grip of the Nazi regime became ever tighter and more frightening as he was coming into adulthood. Bit by bit the life of the Jewish population, which had always considered itself just a normal part of German society, was being restricted, squeezed, and made impossible. Whether or not you were a practicing Jew, and my grandparents and my father were not, you were targeted; impossible for contemporary people who have lived in freedom all their lives to even imagine. Although recent developments have shown that certain situations can easily re-emerge. Eventually the situation in Germany became unbearable, and they made the difficult decision to flee; so, they became refugees. They came from Frankfurt to Amsterdam, the same journey the family of Anne Frank made. They fled to the Netherlands because my grandfather had always been happy to do business with the Dutch. That is how the Netherlands became the country of my birth. The Nazis followed the family not long after though, invading the Netherlands in 1940. They threatened to bomb major Dutch cities, having already flattened the great port city of Rotterdam to show what they were capable of and willing to do. The Dutch surrendered and my father was yet again under the rule of the Nazis he had just fled, and so commenced five years of increasing terror and him having to hide (1940-1945). What made it bad, he would tell me, is that you never knew how long this would last, or whether it would come to an end at all.

This is all part of the story that was unfolding in my mind as an instance of my destiny breaking out of its "attic confinement" – and coming into full view. I was too young

CHAPTER TWENTY-FIVE

to realize all this, therefore it lay in the attic, almost forgotten for decades. It had become just a memory of a piano during moving time when I was just a boy. Yet that piano was capable of eminent music, even as a mere memory, that had to be played, if only metaphorically.

I started to understand that piano in the context of what I knew of my father's upbringing. Add to that the psychologist's understanding that a son inherits his father's dreams, and that children inherit their parents' unlived lives, and we get an ever-unfolding attic treasure.

My father's high school days in Frankfurt, Germany, happened when the city was one of the cultural centers of Europe. This meant that great musicians, great conductors, great singers would come to perform. It was mostly classical music at that time, pop music as a mass cultural phenomenon had not been invented. My father got involved with this musical scene as a boy when he was chosen from local high school kids to sing in some of the great opera productions, used for example in the "street boys' choir" in the opera "Carmen" by Bizet. Along with other youths recruited from local high schools, he landed in great productions with some of the greatest stars of his day. What he got out of working in that heady cultural atmosphere was a very deep and true love for music. For him it was first-hand knowledge, being part of it all, having to study it and perform it. That love became intensified in several ways. That's where the piano comes in.

The young performers, like my father, strangely enough were not paid. I guess at that time they figured that to be part of it all was pay enough in itself, and I might agree! He and his fellow chosen high school buddies would get free tickets to the other great musical events in town. This is where his youthful love for classical music was further deepened. Then there was another important factor which is hard to imagine for us living in an age of internet streaming music. If you wanted to hear the music you loved again, maybe the music you had been directly involved with, there was only one way to do that—go to the music store, buy the sheet music, study it, and play it on the piano. Record players had not yet appeared on the scene. The gramophone, the forerunner of the record player and CD player, was very rare, and unaffordable for most people. With all our music apps, and our variety of other devices, this is hard to imagine. Gramophones were like the super computers of not too long ago, which were available only to big companies and the government; only later the home computer, and then the laptop would make computing available to all.

However, in all of this lay a most wonderful advantage—it required you to study the music in depth. For young people like my father, playing the piano remained the only way to hear the music again. Years later, after I had been born, he bought an early record player as soon as he could afford it; mass production made this possible. The discs were thick as pancakes, heavy and breakable. I broke quite a few of them as a kid, I remember. The player had a steel needle that scratched its way across the surface at an amazing speed of 78 revolutions per minute. My father's direct connection with music was palpable to me and my brother. When he listened to what eventually would be available on the radio and from record stores, he was no passive listener, he lived it. It had entered his bloodstream so to speak. His passion would infect me and my brother and other people as well, since true love for something inspires. His passion was real, and there was nothing of the cultural snob about him. He just loved it, knew it, as it was alive in him. I believe that that unassuming, direct, and genuine enthusiasm, backed

CHAPTER TWENTY-FIVE

up by a lot of knowledge, influenced my approach to art as well. I have always had little patience with the cultural glitterati that inhabit the art world who love to show their sophistication and how high above the common audience they are. My father's sincere and unassuming love of music taught me to love art directly, genuinely, without much fanfare. I cannot forget how he would stand in front of our cumbersomely large radio on Sunday mornings when the classical music program was on (there was no such thing as a "classical station") and, thinking himself unobserved, "conduct" the virtual orchestra coming from the speakers. My brother, who loves classical music in the same way, still does that as well. When you have a father as fascinated by music as my father was, and knowing so much about it as well, you catch something beautiful when you are young. He did not have much of a sense of the visual arts though; that was left up to me to work out for myself.

I have become quite convinced that the rage my father would unleash on me from time to time when he was angry at me, had to do more with the thwarting of his own life's ambitions, than the stupid kid transgressions I engaged in. From somewhere deep in his unconscious that desire for leading the life of music and of art, which necessarily had to be repressed, came spilling out. He most likely saw it coming up in me, and could not abide it, because it reminded him of the forced trajectory of his own life. Seeing in me, his youngest son, the same burgeoning destiny he himself had felt unfolding within him at one time, provoked some deeply buried resentments, or so I have come to believe. My father probably saw in me the same thing that my brother saw—a "damn little artist." I was the carrier of his unfulfilled dreams, and I had been in his eyes no doubt, fortunate enough to be born without all the horrors that he had had to deal with, and which had stopped all normal unfolding of his life. My natural sense of art seemed to irritate him. I do believe that a lot of my own initial reluctance to embrace the life of the artist may have come from encountering that rage and somehow, on a deep level, getting the message that there was something about me that was an anathema to other people, which could set them off. I believe now that I mostly triggered the great disappointment of his life, buried deep within him. When someone is triggered, he or she is not responding to the actual situation or argument, but to some hidden complex deep inside. That part of us then feels provoked and acts out an early hurt. It is not by accident that someone who is angry is said to be "mad" at someone. Anger *is* that: temporary madness.

Once you realize that despite the deep injustice that was done to you, there is a treasure hidden underneath it all, you are face to face with the dawning recognition of your own path! A lot of anger or dismissal directed your way may have its origin exactly in other people's thwarted ambitions. Since being an artist is seen as a desirable position in life, this may happen more often than you think. It may take a long time to be able to gauge it as such, and to deal with it appropriately, but it is a wonderful liberation to be able to do so!

Back to that virtual piano in the attic. It brought a lot of awareness, of my life, of my upbringing, but also of my True Artist destiny. This was especially so when the six-year-old me realized that our piano was not going to be moving with us. I was outraged! It was as if something deep in me had been violated. I threw a temper tantrum of major proportions that took my parents by surprise (temper can be infectious too in a family!) I made a scene, which must have added to the hardships of moving for my poor mother. I would not be surprised if after that, my mother did not

CHAPTER TWENTY-FIVE

have some passing thoughts of not taking me on the move either! However, I did not know how to play the piano, so it was not about being unable to play; it stood for me as an emblem of culture in our home. My disappointment was so profound, so out of proportion I would say, that I can now see that it represented something deep within me. I harangued my parents on and on! I could not for the life of me understand, nor can I now, how people could *not* take their piano with them when they moved. This was sacrilege to me, irreverence, blasphemy! I was only six, but apparently, I was already tuned in to that universe of art which I intuited was my natural habitat. Good for the kid! In that experience, retrieved from my life's attic, I am now able to see my destiny unfolding at its early stages. In that powerful, spontaneous reaction I showed my true colors. To my parents and others, it must have just seemed like the antics of an obstinate difficult kid. But I would compare it to that tender flower pushing through a crack in the asphalt to grow towards the sun. Destiny is not something you can put together in some clever formula. It is revealed in those instances of your experience which have ended up in the attic of your life and that you have finally given appropriate attention. You saved them because you were not quite ready to throw them out. If you go to your attic and do the exciting work of becoming aware of them, you will be able to identify different situations like that, circumstances where your destiny has been taking shape all along. To throw away these experiences from your attic is contrary to your best interests. They are part of the suggestive hints that, at first vaguely, but then more and more definitely, show us the outlines of our fate.

CHAPTER TWENTY-SIX
The Poet of the Two Lines

Another treasure from among my mental attic pieces is the one of "the poet of the two lines." There were periods in my life when the significance of these two lines faded a bit, but they were never completely gone from my mind and remained psychologically active guideposts in my life. But there was more to come from these two lines than I could imagine. Since I did not really memory-hole them, I became interested in investigating it all a bit further and searched for the full poem. Once I found the poem it opened a whole new perspective for me and offered me a more in-depth view of the context from which those lines had come. This cast more light on my own trajectory; far beyond those initial excited insights which had come at me with such power. Knowledge of the author's Ukrainian background and his early twentieth century New York experience all made the experience of his poetry far more meaningful and multilayered for me. A whole series of work flowed from it, though indirectly. Mani's poetry is very straightforward and brilliant in its simplicity, and that straightforwardness and simplicity is something that I have always sought too.

Any of the parts of our mental attic can provide a way of turning skillfulness into mastery if you give it the time and attention they require; I call that "dusting off" and

CHAPTER TWENTY-SIX

"polishing." If you do that they provide much-needed affirmation of your path. This is all part of the process of opening up the channels of creativity, sometimes slowly, sometimes suddenly. That process, once learned, gives unending inspiration; there is then never a lack of "subject matter."

As I told you it was thanks to the sophistication of modern search machines that I was able to meet the poet whose lines had become guidance for me on the path of destiny. The context of his life provided a whole new (and for me, needed) dimension to my understanding of his work. Ultimately the poem speaks for itself, but if you are willing to do some research, some work around it, you may be rewarded with much inspiration. We are the first generation to have nearly all the accumulated knowledge of humankind at our fingertips; we had better make use of our good fortune. A word of caution here because so much is available it may overwhelm us, therefore it is best to start digging a bit where life has grabbed you in some way, the way the lines of the poem did me.

From the information I had gathered, still not knowing the title of the poem, I went on a search for a book that might have the full work in it. I ordered a collection of Yiddish poetry, but the poem was not there, alas. Eventually I came upon *The Penguin Book of Modern Yiddish Verse* (1987), which had a good price as a used book, so I ordered it. A hefty volume it is! And there it was! The poem had both English translation and Hebrew version (which I cannot read). It deserves to be known more fully, because it shows how the poet wrestled meaning from hardship. The journey of inquiry like the one I entered on here, activates the imagination, which is why Carl Jung called this type of process "active imagination." It is a great method indeed, a way of dealing with the imagination; a secret hidden in plain sight.

So, I present to you here the mostly complete poem (minus the first verse) as translated by John Hollander.

> YOU ONLY KNOW ...
> With songs in my breast, the Muse in my heart,
> I went among poets, a poet to be.
>
> When I came, then, among their company,
> Newly fledged from out my shell,
> They lauded and they laureled me,
> Making me one of their number as well.
>
> O Poets, inspired and pale, and free
> As all the winged singers of the air,
> We sang of beauties wild to see
> Like happy beggars at a fair.
>
> We sang, and the echoing world resounded.
> From pole to pole chained hearts were hurled,
> While we gagged on hunger, our sick
> chests pounded:
> More than one of us left this world.
>
> And God, who feedeth even the worm—
> Was not quite lavish with his grace,
> So I crept back, threadbare and infirm,
> To sweat for bread at my working place.
>
> But blessed be, Muse, for your bounties still,
> Though your granaries will yield no bread –
> At my bench, with a pure and lasting will,
> I'll serve you solely until I am dead.

CHAPTER TWENTY-SIX

> In Brownsville, Yehupets, beyond them, even,
> My name shall ever be known, O Muse,
> And I'm not a cobbler who writes, thank heaven,
> But a poet who makes shoes.

The lines as I remembered them were not quite accurate, at least not according to the translation above, but the message was exact and shone through the misremembering. It is said that the proof of a truth inherent in a great story, a great myth, is that it shines through even wrong translations and thoughtless mangling by writers, film makers, poets and comic book artists who use and abuse it. Mani's truth, even in my mangling of his lines, shone through. The actual lines were: "And I am not a cobbler who writes, thank heaven/But a poet who makes shoes."

In that way Mani Leib (also spelled: Leyb) became a real, if unexpected constant companion on my life's journey, an unknown brother of the secret brotherhood, reaching out to me across time. Getting to know him took me decades. He was long gone by the time I met him. It started with just those two lines of his poetry picked up in an unlikely place in downtown Los Angeles. For me those two lines were part of the Ariadne thread I needed to not get lost in the labyrinth of daily life and the creative path of the True Artist. If you do not know the Greek myth of the Ariadne, Theseus, and the Minotaur, half-man, half-bull, at the center of the maze, be sure to look it up. The power of the story will amaze you. Type in "Ariadne's thread" in a search engine, and you may be inspired as I was.

From the poem's two simple lines I had already understood that the poet was a shoe cobbler, a simple craftsman working in New York at the beginning of the 20th century. This was important for me to know because the plain, unpretentious craftsperson has always been close to my heart; I consider myself to be a version of that. It also immediately reminded me of one of the world's greatest philosophers Spinoza, who had to make his simple living as a lens grinder in seventeenth century Holland. He too had fled from his home country as Mani Leib had, because of a similar persecution of Jews in his native Portugal, though they lived in different ages. He ground lenses for glasses put on people's noses, as the poet cobbled shoes put on people's feet. Having a humble profession does not mean that you are not a true poet or a true philosopher or that you could just abandon your destiny because it does not provide you with a living. Being a True Artist, you do what you must. You cobble shoes, grind lenses, design fabrics, produce illustrations, teach college, whatever you do, and you keep the poet, the artist in you alive, and in honor, never forgetting what your true destiny is!

Finally just finding the poet's name, Mani Leib, had a powerful effect on me. It was strange, but giving an actual name to my secret source of power was somehow unsettling, akin to knowing the magician's secret. His words had given a subtle and essential shift to my life as an artist, and I cherished that as some personal treasure, and I felt protective of its subtle meaning. Now it became real in a different way.

After finding the poet, knowing more of his work and some of the history in which it is embedded, I do what I do with all attic treasures, even though this was never a forgotten treasure as such. It is a most exciting process that Carl Jung calls "amplification." It is like throwing a pebble in a lake and becoming entranced with the ripples endlessly expanding and then slowly disappearing. This is a process where, in a very personal way, you begin to feel out the different dimensions of something that has attracted your attention. While we are dealing here with memories, it can also be dreams, musings, sudden insights, or other things you sense have hidden dimensions that you, as an adventurer, want to explore. Now the mere memory became an actual page in a thick volume on my desk. Amplification can mean turning up the volume on things, making it louder, but here it meaning is more akin to its original meaning in Latin—to make larger, to make more abundant. As I delve deeper into the poem, I am not trying to explicate the poem, as a literary critic would, I am trying to find a way into the wisdom embedded in it which gripped the young man I was with just a few of its lines. It is as if finding an exciting piece of furniture or ceramics and wanting to know what worldview produced such a kind of work.

As I reflect on the poem, I always keep in mind what the occasion was for me to become acquainted with it; I was just grabbing lunch at a simple sandwich stand in the Los Angeles fashion district. I was a common fabric designer, unsure of my life's trajectory, unsure whether I had "what it takes."

With that in mind, I took my first tentative steps into the poem. The first few lines, though they are beautiful and obviously pregnant lines, I find too obscure and not immediately inviting further exploration, maybe later. Then Mani continues with lines that find immediate resonance within me.

"With songs in my breast, the Muse in my heart, I went among poets, a poet to be."

Here he speaks of what he found within himself, a natural gift, "songs," and inspiration. Then he speaks of seeking out those who also carried songs "in their breasts," and he did so because he thought it would solidify his search to become a poet, or as he says, "a poet to be."

THE POET OF THE TWO LINES

For countless huddled masses of the world, New York was the symbol of freedom, but it proved to be for most more a harsh and unforgiving environment. Still, it was infinitely better than what he had left behind. Mani and his fellow poets discovered that the city was not exactly ready to welcome Jewish refugees from a barely known (though very large) part of the Soviet Union (the former USSR, the Union of Soviet Socialist Republics). Add to this that Mani and his compatriots insisted on writing in Yiddish. Yiddish consists of concepts and idioms taken from different languages from Eastern and Central European sources. It also incorporates Hebrew and Aramaic, but it is mainly German. It is no "official" language of any kind, and 18th century Jews, eager to integrate in their new homeland, would dismiss it as barbaric jargon. However, it was already a shared-identity language with the Jewish populations in countries in Eastern and Central Europe and the Slavic countries. Whatever else is true, Yiddish is an intense, direct, alive language, full of emotion and highly expressive. Though its literature has been disseminated for centuries, it has stayed mostly within its original ethnic and cultural boundaries.

Mani and his poet brothers seem to have been fired with the higher purpose of making Yiddish poetry, a poetry in a "lowly language", as official as any other poetry; they too were after transformation: turning their base materials into gold. Since I got Mani's complete poem from *The Penguin Book of Modern Yiddish Verse*, published by a well-known publishing house in 1987, I can only surmise that their higher purpose was fulfilled. A large publishing company would not bring out a thick hard cover compilation of obscure poetry if it were not seen as viable literary expression. There are many instances of such a higher purpose

CHAPTER TWENTY-SIX

being fulfilled posthumously. Penguin Books has done us a great service.

It is hard for us to imagine what moral courage and character Mani and his friends must have had for this kind of enterprise. In general, we can say that an overriding goal, a higher purpose with our artistry, sanctifies and energizes our creativity. It certainly extends beyond such things as becoming popular on Instagram or in the gallery scene.

Our own times often see a higher purpose only in terms of serving some political or ideological ends. True Artists, however, know in their bones that a higher purpose comes from our deeper selves. The deeper self, below the level of rational thought, is from where artists connect with others. However antithetical this may sound, the higher coming from the deeper, it is exactly that which produces what we call "culture." It is the expression of what lives in the collective mind as filtered through the individual mind and being of the True Artist. Often the artist him—or herself is not even sure of what he or she is filtering. Mythology originates in like manner.

Recently I found another example of a band of poets like Mani and his friends; poets using a scorned language, having a higher purpose and intend on making their presence felt. And it would connect with one of my examples of a True Artist. I was in Arles, France and came across a bit of history of the Provençal poets. In the region of Provençe (literally "province") in France, the people have had their own language, their own dialect of French, "Provençal," for centuries. The French government, to squelch any separatist movement, in the 19th century, outlawed the use of it. It was simply not to be spoken or written anymore! This was of course the kind of manipulation that governments like to engage in throughout history to increase and maintain their power. A special language for a part of the country challenges the centralized power and cannot and will not be allowed. The history of China first united under emperor Qin Shi Huang is another example. To unite the several competing kingdoms which he had conquered into one nation, now known as "China," he instituted one language to replace all the different languages spoken. He did so under the motto, "Burn the books, bury the scholars." And he meant it, burning the books, and burying hundreds of scholars, alive!

In Provençe the situation was not quite as bad as that, but the French government did go hard against the scholars and the poets, the cultural exponents of the Provençal. A group of poets, like Mani Leib and his cohorts, stood up against this tyrannical move. Under the leadership of the poet Frédéric Mistral, they formed a protest movement and by means of their poetry railed against the edicts of the central government.[1]

Here my amplification of these historical facts took another interesting turn for me and became part of my bigger "destiny project." In Arles, a city in Provençe, you can now see a statue of Mistral on the town's square. This statue is however in a very interesting place. It is literally just a few steps away from the restaurant that Van Gogh made famous with his work, "The Night Café." Mistral and Vincent were contemporaries, working around the same time, though I'm not sure they ever met. In my mind Van Gogh, as a one-man band, connected with Mistral and his band of rebel poets in a most peculiar and masterful way, which finds expression in Mistral's statue being so close to an outdoor café that people from all over the world know about through Van Gogh's

---

1 Mistral would eventually get the Nobel prize for literature.

CHAPTER TWENTY-SIX

work. To me they are indeed like spiritual brothers of the secret brotherhood, united in a surprising way.

Mani and his band of poet friends, like Mistral and his own version of it, certainly stacked the deck against themselves. Mistral by advocating for a banned language, Mani by insisting on Yiddish, when even the Jewish community itself did not give much credence to Yiddish as a literary language; something he acknowledges, painfully, in the poem.

Coming to know the history of the poet and his companions and additional analogous situations in different parts of the world and different periods of history, as part of the so-called "amplification" process, was one way for me to become aware of the True Artist's path, including the painful aspects of it. In the stories that flowed from the two lines that I chanced upon long ago, I encountered the True Artist's identity as destiny. From the new insights I gained from delving deeper into the stories of courageous poets and artists, I became aware of the weight of my own natural disposition and my choice to follow it. I would not have been able to explain it at that time, but through the work that flowed from the revelation over the years, I was able to realize the extent of its truth. I like the meaning of the word destiny or "fate" from the original Latin meaning "that which has been spoken." It fits with seeing my "fate" revealed in the words of a poet. It was "spoken" in poetry and does not have to be spoken in the form of a scientific formula, a psychological diagnosis, or as evidence in a court case. It serves as an illumination of the meaning of life. To co-opt an old saying, "Art has its reasons, that reason cannot understand."[1]

---

[1] The heart has its reasons that reason does not know about – "Le cœur a ses raisons que la raison ne connaît point" – Blaise Pascal

Back to the poem. When it says, "With songs in my breast, the Muse in my heart..." we see this radical proponent of Yiddish literature mentioning an ancient Greek goddess, the Muse. This is surprising, is it not? How can we understand this without getting too deeply into Greek mythology? I studied and taught enough mythology to know how extensive and complex the subject is, and what a fool's errand it is to try and catch it in some simple explanations. I can say however that I was certainly closer to Greek mythology than to Yiddish culture and had probably picked up some of the unspoken disdain for it. I could not relate well to it, though I liked its energetic and almost pugnacious character, as you find in the pre-eminent Yiddish writer Sholem Aleichem. But now I had to come to terms with the lines that had shaken lose my sense of destiny, which I now realized had come from a Yiddish perspective. I had learned from one of my earlier mentors never to dismiss anything just because it makes you feel uncomfortable, so I allowed myself to delve deeper into it. Of course, that is also part of the "amplification" process and as such promises a possible opening of inspiration, a path to imaginative possibilities. And so I discovered that modern Yiddish literature had been spearheaded in the late 19th century by some writers who are now rather well-known,[1] and that it was indeed great literature. This was around the same time that Mani and his cohorts were writing. The writers in Yiddish speak with a stunning directness and unvarnished realism born from harsh realities. They married this with a sense of irony, humor, and a good amount of irreverence, which was, as I understand it, a way of overcoming the pain of those realities. This is the

---

[1] Mendele Seforim, I. L. Peretz and Sholem Aleichem (the latter also, like Mani, from Ukraine)

True Artist at work. These qualities became the hallmarks of Yiddish culture, and so potent that some of it seeped into the general culture. Yiddish is so direct, plain, and exactly to the point that words like "chutzpah" for a cheeky audacity-beyond-audacity, has become well known to many. Other words like "schmuck" for jerk, or "schmooze" for small talk, are now just part of common language usage. The English dictionary defines them as "Yiddishisms."

How does the Greek goddess, the Muse, fit into this? We must delve a bit into mythology here (but let us be careful, because it can become all-consuming!). The Muse is one of nine sisters known as the inspirational goddesses for artists, poets, writers, and scientists. They are in fact considered the very source of poetry and mythology itself. The Muse represents that larger dimension of inspiration of which our individual creativity is just a part. The Greeks had a keen sense of how things fit together, the worldly and the other-worldly. In no other religion, culture, or mythology that I know of, is there a figure comparable to the Muse. I know of no other gods or goddesses or mythological figures that "preside" over the whole spectrum of creativity[1]. Being embodied in a celestial figure tells us that creativity is not the clever inventiveness of an individual mind, but a gift from a higher (or deeper) source. Yet here I was confronted with my new old Yiddish friend throwing me a curve ball with his allusion to Greek mythology. By invoking the Muse, Mani affirms that larger dimension of his work which, even with his predilection for things Yiddish, he cannot find represented in any other way. Even the secularists amongst us acknowledge that creativity often hits us from a place we

---

[1] The Hindu goddess Saraswati comes close to being the same as goddess of the arts, poetry, music, language and culture, as well as learning.

do not know. "Out of the blue" we call it. We do know that it is not something that we can somehow force. Like sexual attraction, it cannot be manufactured on demand. There are ways to set the mood, to set the right conditions, but ultimately it is beyond our control. We give it less spiritual names, like "being in the zone," or we ascribe it to the secretion of hormones of some sort, or we talk about the collective unconscious and the creative imagination, but it all speaks of something larger than ourselves, something of which we are only a part. We may be able to detect which way the winds blow but it is still up to us to adjust our sails, to catch that wind, and set the course. No wonder we often get blown off course like Odysseus in Homer's Odyssey.

Still, what does a poet committed to Yiddish do calling on a Greek goddess? The Jews have had a long and troubled relationship with ancient Greek thought and traditions, together named: Hellenism. Mani thus steps into a long-running controversy involving Jewish life and history. There were some great Jewish thinkers and scholars who were Hellenists, while others rejected Greek thought out of hand, as something to be avoided. The Greek tradition, although the foundation of Western civilization and more, was never an easy fit for the Jews. Christianity embraced part of Greek philosophy, mainly through the work of people like Thomas Aquinas (13th century), who strove to show how Greek thought, though centuries before Jesus' appearance, had somehow prepared the way for Christ's teachings. But they did not and could not extend to adopting the pantheon of Greek divinities. As a poet in Yiddish, Mani is already on the fringes of the poetic world, but with this allusion to Greek divinity he is on the fringes of Jewish life as well, and since neither one of them is that large to begin with, he is in a minority of a minority. He is boldly proclaiming his

CHAPTER TWENTY-SIX

isolation, which can be an important and difficult part of the True Artist's existence. There are however few more direct ways of saying that you are a committed artist, doing something which is essential to your being, being a True Artist, than saying that you are "serving the Muse."

The place dedicated to art we call a muse-um and in that way acknowledge it as the home of the Muse. The verb "to muse," in typical modern fashion, has been de-natured and stripped of its spiritual dimension and relegated only to thinking. To muse, according to the dictionary, is to think deeply, to ponder, to turn over in one's mind. But, to muse actually means to step into that larger creative dimension away from the immediate and the current, with its incessant claims on us.

Mani Leib invokes the Muse to tell us in a simple poet's words that he is dedicated above all to his art and to his poetry; that he is definitely a True Artist. Appealing to the divine realm, he is saying that "my task is holy," as Hermann Hesse puts it in one of his stories. He speaks of his disappointment that God did not see fit to provide him with the necessities of life to better serve his Muse. Having to do manual work, hard work in the hard world, seems to be his fate. The Dutch poet who said, "...and the poets seem strange, because they don't really work," did not take into account that poets have to do work outside of their service to the Muse. Mani shows his cultural isolation, of which the poet Rilke speaks when he says in *The Poet's Guide to Life*, that the artist may be denied his or her proper place in their own era. This is part of destiny. You may want to change it because things are so difficult, but by destiny we mean exactly that it is set and cannot be otherwise. Once aware of your own deepest convictions, you can only support them with the tender care of your mastery.

> "And God, who feedeth even the worm–
> Was not quite lavish with his grace,
> So I crept back, threadbare and infirm,
> To sweat for bread at my working place."

Disappointed in God, the artist does not become disloyal to his Muse. He may have to come to the realization that hardships are part of the dimensions of the True Artist's life, as we have alluded throughout. Somewhat plaintively, he relates that his poet compatriots are "inspired and pale," a painful realization no doubt. But he also adds, and here is the True Artist aware of a destiny speaking, that they are "free." Dedication is not "free" of risk and the True Artist destiny takes moral courage to pursue. It would have been quite understandable had he said, "Okay, New York, you got me. This is not the place to create Yiddish poetry. We are outnumbered in so many ways, and even our fellow Jews don't much appreciate us. What were we thinking?" But no, his mission was larger than that, and it was not "thinking" that got them into that predicament; it was a sense of dedication to destiny, infinitely more than something merely thought out.

"But blessed be, Muse, for your bounties still," he continues. showing that he is committed, dedicated. Then declares boldly that, "At my bench, with pure and lasting will, I'll serve you solely until I am dead."

He does not demand that the Muse or God provide him with what he wants just because he is such a dedicated guy; he is willing to serve. There is that one central reality for him. Then, to show his determination, he says, "until I am dead." But, being a True Artist, he is also desirous of recognition, because why would a poet write, unless he is reaching out and wants to connect to readers? Therefore,

CHAPTER TWENTY-SIX

he finds it important to tell us that "My name shall ever be known, O Muse..."

It seems a surprising bit of boasting, just when he got us to think that he was such a humble servant (and that is what endears him to me), because this too is part of the True Artist's mental make-up, the vacillation between swagger and humility. You got to have both, and it is a never-ending pendulum swing. This he then plays out in the poem, when his grand pronouncement is given a twist of typical Yiddish irony and humorous self-deprecation:

"In Brownville, Yehupets, beyond them even..." Yehupets is a fictional name given to Kyiv, the capital of Ukraine, by Sholem Aleichem. While Kyiv (or Kiev) is now a name that has become widely known because of an unfortunate war, it was then little known to most of the world. It is also meant to indicate a transitional place, something between a "shtetl" and a modern city. The "shtetl" was that small village already mentioned, where poor Jews lived in harsh conditions under threat of recurring pogroms and it certainly was not a place to further anybody's fame; not the way New York or Hollywood might be. In a romanticized version, the shtetl has become more of an iconic presence in the public's mind because of the musical "Fiddler on the Roof," and its movie version. However, the shtetl no longer exists and is a relic of history.

Then Mani Leib adds, "...beyond them even..." which is a statement of a True Artist desirous of his destiny being sanctified. Who can dispute that this sanctification did not happen? That his pronouncement was spurious? Here I am in twenty-first century America, distant in time, essence, and calling, availing myself of his poem to write what is closest to my own heart! Is this not what a True Artist's true mission is all about? He somehow persisted, he somehow "beat out his exile," the way Ezra Pound puts it; the exile being his relative obscurity. The call one hears, vaguely, inside, and then more and more distinctly, is not necessarily about one's own time or place, although we all want to be seen in the hot shot galleries or be on the best—seller list. It can be a reaching out beyond time and place to unknown others who, though unknown, are closer than we think. Mani chooses his words to pronounce his supposed glory as a poet, which upon closer inspection may not be quite so glamorous. Even artists who have achieved great fame have been known to recoil from it, because it threatened their sense of destiny as much, or more, than obscurity could.

After he renews his vows to the Muse, with "a pure and lasting will" and "'til death do us part," he pens the lines that became a lifesaver to a struggling young artist who was often afraid of failing in his mission. Here they are again in the way I remembered them:

"I am not a cobbler who writes poetry, thank God,
But a poet who cobbles shoes."

That is a little bit different from John Hollander's translation of the poem in the Penguin edition. Translations of poetry are delicate things. Since I do not read Hebrew or Yiddish, I cannot be sure. The way I remembered it as "Thank God" is a bit stronger in my opinion than "thank heaven" which seems more non-committal. Its essence remains the same to me.

I am not sure what else Mani's poetry and that of his other Yiddish poets have to tell me, but I am open to it. I am not a scholar but follow certain themes in my life, opened up by the attic treasures I come upon. My secret compatriot on my life's journey who has been alongside me for quite a while now and through research now easily available on the internet, has shown his face, made himself known to me,

CHAPTER TWENTY-SIX

and gotten me interested in the many other things I just wrote about. I met him through the power of poetry, his art, and he was one of those who taught me what a True Artist is. And all by way of a "lowly sandwich stand." This way Mani is part of the secret brotherhood of True Artists for me. It was a gradual getting to know him, extending over the many years which I now call, appropriately, the "Mani years!" Here was someone telling me, "I understand you, you are not alone, you have compatriots, people who know what you are all about." He is not a world-famous poet, but his work is important; it has the power to speak to us directly.

Everyone who picks up this book has their own version of this story; if you look for it, you will find it. It will be different, but it is there. Pick up the thread from anywhere and follow it to its origins. If you say, "I can't find it," you are not looking hard enough! Or it may speak of things you do not want to consider, think about, know about. Not yet at least. We do not want to tarnish the happiness we find in creating art, but eventually find that we cannot confine our artmaking to just seeking happiness in the making of it. It necessarily has a more challenging side, which we must acknowledge if we are indeed to follow our destiny as True Artists. There are enough biographies of good and great artists to alert us to some of the harder realities. Sometimes it is just a sentence in one of those biographies that we easily pass over, but which contains a world of meaning. In a recent biography I read there was this almost throwaway line that the artist "also" suffered periods of depression after having done some of her greatest work; then the book blithely went on about the greatness of her work. But if you stop and think about it and examine it a bit closer, you realize that this was a major challenge to the artist, one that had to be overcome with great effort, and most likely something she struggled with time and time again. But most of us just want to see the glory aspect of the story, without wanting to consider the converse side of it; although there are also those who like to obsess about the darker drama of the creative life. This is the drama that inspires moviemakers, and we should not dismiss it or suppress awareness of its reality. But it is also important for us to know that a True Artist's life may be uneventful, "un-cinematic" yet deeply meaningful.

CHAPTER TWENTY-SEVEN
Loneliness

Mani showed us that there is a certain loneliness that is an unavoidable part of the path of the True Artist. Coming to understand it as a natural part of my destiny was important. I had to get over seeing it as some personal failing, a character flaw of some sort, may be even a "disorder." It often needs a thoughtful sorting through the different aspects of this loneliness, so we do not suffer needlessly. Good therapy can be a real help, and I am certainly a proponent of it, but I also know that not every therapist is able to understand the artist and may try to "normalize" the True Artist client, helping them to adjust to being a "regular" person. This is why the poet Rilke said that he was afraid mental health professionals may not just get rid of his devils but of his angels as well.

A person of vision and passion tends to stand alone. Someone like that often makes others feel uncomfortable, just by being who he or she is. And often the person him— or herself can be uncomfortable with it as well because it has its price. Rather than a full acceptance of one's path, the True Artist may experience a sense of fear and inferiority, in face of the world. There is an interiority that is part of the True Artist path which stands in sharp contrast to the action-oriented, extraverted world around him or her. I remember some personal notes of Hermann Hesse to that effect, which gave me a needed sense of self-acceptance, and a sense of not being alone. He was working then on a book that would eventually garner worldwide acclaim, *Siddhartha*. He was sitting at his writing desk in his home in Switzerland looking out at the world, struck by a sense of futility. Out there he writes, he saw big buildings going up, the city buzzing with action, and on his desk lay a few pages with words, a slender manuscript, which he felt as being a somewhat vulnerable and insignificant presence. I would go to the university library to read his notes in the original German, because it had not been translated (yet?), and I remember feeling I had a special pipeline to some truths there and to a fellow artist. The exact words do not matter, but what it spoke of was that painful sense of feeling inconsequential. We often feel this kind of vulnerability doing our work. And yet Hesse's book, that small little manuscript, a bundle of pages with words, would fly to all corners of the earth, and into millions of minds. It spoke to those in the high rises he saw being built, but also to people in the simple farmhouses he adored, and many in distant countries, who read it in translation. The furious activity of the city which had made him feel insignificant lay tamed in his slender pages.

This is a challenging feature of our path and may take a long time to get into the proper perspective. It is a necessary reality. Anthony Storr's book *Solitude* does a wonderful job of exploring how loneliness may be transformed into solitude, a productive creative space rather than a painful sense of isolation. Loneliness transformed into solitude can mean living in the bustling world, fully engaged, but keeping an inner sanctum of tranquility amid it all.

CHAPTER TWENTY-SEVEN

"O why was I born with a different face?
Why was I not born like the rest of my race?
When I look, each one starts! when I speak, I offend;
Then I'm silent & passive & lose every Friend."

William Blake

CHAPTER TWENTY-EIGHT
Mastery Revisited

After having dealt with some of the issues of the True Artist's life sparked by a couple of my own personal "attic treasures," we can look at that important pillar of our destiny—mastery—again and give it more dimension. Mastery is forged in the solitude we just touched upon, in the cauldron of the inner realm. It is a mysterious, organic coming together of different parts of our personality around an expertise that has been consolidated, through continuous practice, into a solid core. Expertise is quite straightforward, mastery is not. Expertise reaches a level where it becomes second nature, a stage where it has sunk deeply into us and is now one of our natural abilities, quite like riding a bike; once you know how, you no longer think about it, you just do it. In mastery, insight, intuition, thought, and deep imagination—what we called "poetics"—naturally connect with and direct that technical knowledge that has become second nature. Elements of mastery appear at all stages of skill gathering. Master art teacher Robert Henri in his book *The Art Spirit*, alludes to that when he says that one should always practice as a poet. He is one who believes as I do, that we cannot put off acquiring mastery until we are technically proficient but should make it part of our project from the beginning, and at every stage. In fact, he assumes that it is the impulse to mastery that should guide our acquiring of technical ability; an intense "need" to say something literally demands that we are proficient in what we do.

Mastery comes from those deeper, wider parts of us, which we catch glimpses of now and then, but too often dismiss. In an age filled with sense stimulation, getting to that deeper, wider part is not easy. Here the more meditation-oriented disciplines have a lot to teach us. The mastery of the True Artist is not in service of a race to the top of the art world, but to infuse the world with dignity and meaning. This is what we call "tending the flame of culture." The True Artist is dedicated to keeping it going, which is why we call True Artists "keepers of the flame."

THE ALCHEMY OF MASTERY

Tending the flame is a basic and literal aspect of alchemy. Mostly misunderstood, alchemy is probably the first truly global phenomenon, appearing in all corners of the earth. It seems to be a natural drive in human beings for a road to transformation. Long before worldwide communications were possible, almost all cultures had their version of it. We see it in India, Europe, China, Africa, and the Arab world. Most people associate it with some mystical, unscientific forerunner of the science of chemistry. However, chemistry had already come into being, contrary to the common knowledge on the subject. Alchemy was and is a curious confluence of deeply psychological exploration, spiritual pursuits, and a practical, though perplexing, materialistic, near scientific exploration, a dive into the technology of transformation and transmutation. At the center of the alchemist's workshop was a fire as shown in many old prints, paintings, and in their writings; it was meant to heat the elements used in experiments for the supposed transmutation of base metals into gold. It was supposed to be kept always going, and at just the proper temperature. This was an essential part of the alchemist's preoccupations. The writings about it are often obscure, referring to things only obliquely. It was Carl Jung who brought it to the attention of the contemporary world by studying the old manuscripts. Being an admirer of Jung, I must admit that at first, I was unhappy that he did that, because I felt that it made him look like one of those mystery-mongers that I do not appreciate. However, he won me over, and though I am by no means an expert on the subject, Jung's approach has given me wonderful insights into the creative process. The ancient Greeks, Chinese, and Eastern Indians referred to what we call "alchemy" literally as "The Art." It was always a radically creative endeavor, separate from and parallel to the officially sanctioned truths upheld by society and its religious institutions. Because it challenged the powers that be, its practice included the art of hiding in plain sight. Their manuscripts are most perplexing and obscure for that very reason, but with some of the clues revealed by Jung, they start to make wonderous sense and give insights into the "alchemical aspects" of art making. Jung realized that the alchemists' writings were really about spiritual transformation.

The fire at the center of that "Art" is what interests me here, because in all the very perplexing writings and coded messages that the alchemists left behind, this remains constant— keeping the fire burning at all times—the flame that somehow heated the material transformations attempted. It is not something that you kindle, let go out, and reignite. The world-renowned French poet, Arthur Rimbaud, connects alchemy to creating art. He says: "True alchemy lies in this formula: 'Your memory and your senses are but the nourishment of your creative impulse.'" Quite rightfully he saw creating art as a process of transformation, and that is how I understand it as well. We spoke of that when we mentioned poetics as part of the True Artist's endeavor and discussed Aristotle's insights. Poets use the same words we all use but transform them into deeper meaning by the manipulations they perform. Painters—using what is merely colored mud called "paint"—have created some of the most penetrating and beautiful statements of the human condition, thus transmuting the base materials into deep meaning. Computer artists use light and its properties to create the semblance of things that do not exist, but rather exist only as light wave patterns on electronic devices. This is in line with our understanding that all of life's experiences serve as base materials for our art, what the alchemists call the "prima materia," the base materials of everyday experience. That is what goes into the fire, the fire of transformation.

KEEPERS OF THE FLAME

Oscar Jenniger's designation of artists as "Keepers of the Promethean flame," shows the artist as tending the fire of civilization, also indicating that the fire is "of the gods" and not of the individual psyche. While this fire may burn bright at times, it most often flickers in the winds of threatening change. True Artists, by keeping the flame constant, are the ones who transmute the base elements of our lives into what we recognize as culture. Because the alchemists were so insistent on this part of their work, though rather cryptic about the reasons for it, the perceived necessity of keeping the fire going, and going just so, works well for us as a metaphor for our own destiny. We all do it in our individual manner, and that too is a characteristic of alchemy;

it was never a collective endeavor but an individual effort, yet part of a larger societal movement. Arthur Rimbaud's understanding of the creative process as a sacrificial fire into which we toss the plain elements of our individual lives is close to the sacrifice to the Muse of which Mani Leib speaks of in his poem as well. Our normal human experiences are the fuel for our creativity, transforming them into much more than they appear at first blush.

For us, the failure to tend the fire comes in the form of constant seductions to abandon our projects. The fire of creativity is a difficult thing to manage. Flare ups can be followed by let downs and we become assailed by doubts. Sometimes a sense of futility floods in, a feeling that the world has more important things to do, or that the world is beyond redemption, or that our efforts amount to very little. Remember Hesse's *Siddhartha*, that slender "unimportant" manuscript that became a worldwide literary hit. We saw how at some time it lay on his writing desk as a paltry pile of papers. The result of giving in to that "seduction of futility" as an artist friend of mine calls it, is within us and yet, strangely enough, a luxury that we cannot afford; we must keep constant watch on the fire. To the True Artist it may seem that the world is set up to extinguish the fire. This is true. For the True Artist the pursuit of mastery is the paramount way we fight back and keep the fire of creativity going at the proper temperature, trying to avoid those flare ups and let downs. In the deeper recesses of our mind, the allegiance to something greater than the thing we are working on at the time always remains. Long ago I read wonderful stories about a powerful ruler in ancient India, someone of tremendous power and responsibility, who was yet a True Artist, a poet, a painter, and a musician, able to transform his worldly power and responsibilities into art. Though rare,

CHAPTER TWENTY-EIGHT

this is an example of how the original inspiration of the True Artist's life is not necessarily corrupted by the seductions of power; and that, of course, is its greatness. The one who said that if he had to be condemned to hell, he hoped that he could take his writing materials with him, was a True Artist. Thomas Merton was a great Catholic mystic and inspirational writer. At the point of entering the monastery he was willing to "be obedient" and give up his writing but was dissuaded by the abbot. That allowed Merton's great contributions to come to us.

CHAPTER TWENTY-NINE
The Wonderful Wizard of Oz

Another hint about the True Artist destiny came to me from the author of *The Wonderful Wizard of Oz*; not so much the story itself as the story around its inception and eventual success. As I already mentioned, I had the good fortune of delving into the life of its creator, Frank Baum (1856-1919), when I was asked to design a serious first exhibit on his life for the Samuel Goldwyn Company in Hollywood. That project became an intriguing exploration of the shape and destiny of the True Artist. While my attention was taken up with the details of the Oz stories, and how to bring them and Baum's story to life, I got a valuable education. Baum certainly was a True Artist; his stories, though highly entertaining were aiming at something deeper.

Early Hollywood was one of those bustling nerve centers of creativity that pop up from time to time in history and in very different forms. Not unlike Renaissance Florence (Italy) in the 14th and 15th century, it was a magnet for the creative and would-be creative types bewitched by the newly discovered power of the movie. It must have been an irresistible magnet for those wanting to be heard, and those having something to say. Baum was of the latter variety. Among the glamour obsessed, and the power player elites running Hollywood (my great grand uncle Carl Laemmle, founder of

Universal Studios, being one of them), he cut a lonely but eventually significant figure. He got his start writing the Oz stories (a whole series of books) in humble fashion. Starting out as mere bedtime stories for his children, he charmingly revealed that he had the feeling that when he was telling his little sons stories, he was one of them. He was, it is obvious, in touch with that inner part of us that never grows old, that playful part that remains curious and amazed at life. The "inner child" as some psychologists like to call it, is really that first manifestation of who we are supposed to be, and it remains with us. A child does not have the sophisticated words, nor thoughts to give it proper expression, but experiences it directly, and intensely. The child knows! So, when we talk about 'the inner child' in relation to the True Artist destiny, we are merely indicating the first appearance of a sense of destiny that stays with us over the course of our life time. The French poet Charles Baudelaire refers to that when he says, "[G]enius is nothing more nor less than childhood recaptured at will." By this he does not mean some kind of regression, but an acknowledgement that our first knowing is fundamental and proves to be essential. The True Artist at work is like a child at play but with the sophistication of an adult managing the whole affair. We saw this in how from the early bedtime stories he invented for his kids, Frank Baum consciously set out to create American fairy tales. He knew that fairy tales are carriers of essential values, and ways to pass them on. "The Wizard of Oz" would eventually gain the iconic status of a quintessential American fairy tale with the unavoidable archetype of the American psyche, the "orphan" at its center, just what he set out to do. But it gained its status as such only when television had become ubiquitous and made it a yearly family event and thus cemented the story's place in the collective consciousness of generations of Americans. Are we now going to say that he failed as an artist, just because his movie company eventually went bust and he did not live to see the eventual victory of his vision?! Part of the True Artist's life can be contending with such a fate, or of not being understood or appreciated. It is often said that artists are ahead of their times. However, I believe that those with vision are very much *of* their own time, but see more deeply into it, seeing what is not yet visible to others. Men and women of vision see what may come more fully into view much later.

It is important to note, that we can also see a less productive understanding and actual inversion of the above truth when artists mistake not being understood or appreciated as meaning that they are ahead of their time. You may be sure that it usually means that their mastery is not yet up to the level of what they have to say. It is a common misconception which only diverts us from our path. We must seek to connect with people, whether that audience is large or small, living now or later. The entertainment industry tries to gain an audience for its products (and needs it because of the prohibitive costs of movie making) by appealing to what the audience wants, but the True Artist tries to connect on a deeper and less obvious level, though his or her art may of course also be most appealing to an audience of contemporaries.

CHAPTER THIRTY
The Practical True Artist

Even with much thought on the matter, we must also find a practical approach to all of this; thinking only gets us part of the way. We must first get a sense of what our adventure in life is all about, which is the essence of this book. We must get some grip on our destiny, whether we stand at the beginning or are well on the way. Our destiny is often lost in plain sight because of how our contemporary world is structured. But once we have gotten hold of the issues involved, we want to know how to go about getting mastery. There is a time for praxis, a time to get practical.

A True Artist destiny is a very individual matter, and therefore there is no one right way for all. As we said in the beginning, there is no definite path, no manual for how to be a True Artist, but there is something like a right approach to it all, complimented with an awareness of the detours that might be avoided. This is why it is important to understand the issues involved. We have already established that an essential feature of the True Artist is mastery, and that mastery is always built around a solid core of technical proficiency. We can look at least at one of the ways of getting that proficiency, one good enough to allow for our individuality to come through, and which is certainly time tested. It is a method that has allowed so many to advance on the path, both in pursuing the essential path of destiny and allowing for personal idiosyncrasies to be part of it. It is exactly those idiosyncrasies that make our work interesting. Idiosyncrasies are gold to a contemporary audience. I like that aspect of pop music where it is often not the perfectly smooth voice of the professional singer that interests us today, but that occasional raw edge in a voice that makes it compelling, individual, and gives us a feeling of the presence of who is singing. That is a feature of the spirit of our times.

The question becomes what technique to pursue? The appropriate field is always the one you feel naturally most attracted to. Some of the suggestive hints of this book have come from my own sense of natural attraction, how I found that and how I dealt with it. That natural inclination is the right place to start in the age we live in. In former times things were more circumscribed, as were our lives, and one followed in the path of the masters who set the course of culture, as one followed in the footsteps of one's parents. Often the subject matter was pretty much set as well, mostly a shared spiritual tradition as seen in Christian art, Buddhist, and Indian art; or observations of everyday life as depicted in Japanese woodblock prints of the Edo period, or 17th century Dutch painting. Nowadays, we have the task of finding our own way which, although we are drowning in information and images, remains a major challenge. Scenes of everyday life have become a suffocating presence because of the ubiquitous smart phone which "records" everything everywhere. I believe however, that in the face of that too, the "poetics" dimension remains, where we face the same task as generations before us: to distill essences from the common place, to transform the accidental into the essential. Individual destinies may or may not be aligned with prevailing cultural currents, may be lagging or advanced,

CHAPTER THIRTY

may even be in opposition to them, but the task remains the same: transformation.

If you are not one of those who just knew from the get-go what was right for you, the task becomes searching for your natural gift. Often it lies buried under layers of inner doubts or external expectations that you have been trying to live up to for too long. It must be something you know naturally and intimately, "in your gut" as they say. Some people have a feel for mechanical things and gravitate towards that. Others, like me, lack that talent, and have other "gut competencies." As one more suggestive hint, I will tell you of unearthing my own "gut competency."

Let me share a challenge I faced. I realized that I had always naturally been a songwriter. I was writing songs organically and spontaneously long before I could play any instrument or realized that was what I was doing. I just did it, and then became aware that I was doing it. I invented my own musical notations to remember the melodic lines I had put together in my head, while out in the world, or just before going to sleep. I was always inwardly busy getting lyrics just right, the melody just right. I am still doing it. So that would be a natural place to start, right? Only after did I learn to play the guitar, and well enough to get my point across and make it enjoyable for people to listen to. That was my natural thing you might say. I had to come to the realization that it was also part of the spirit of the times, that everybody was picking up a guitar to join the blossoming pop music culture. You have no doubt seen people playing "air guitar" where they mimic the moves of a solo rock guitarist. This is a wonderful fantasy but not an indication of a natural inclination, especially if it never translates into actual playing. I took some guitar lessons, but the older woman who taught them could not steer my contemporary inclinations, but at least I engaged in actual playing and singing. At the time, playing and singing somewhat satisfied the creative hunger in me.

Now we get to the next layer, an important part of the process for me and many others. Though I loved learning new things on the guitar, new chords and new finger picking styles, and other things brought to my attention by friends (YouTube videos on how to play did not exist then). Whatever I learned, I immediately used in making songs. Yet, I also found that I was not really "a musician." A songwriter is not necessarily the same as a musician; he or she fits more in the category of the old troubadours, poets of some sort who went around singing their songs in most more ancient societies in the world. Some song writers are great musicians as well, but that is not necessary for song writing. I realized that I did not have it in me to become a guitar virtuoso like I saw some of my friends develop into. Though I became a good songwriter and player, and I have kept it up while others put their guitars in their real attics, I know that it was, as I indicated before, one of those planets revolving around my core interest. I had the distinct feeling that I was not doing the hard work that would satisfy the calls of my destiny. However, before doing my daily writing on this book, I did what I do daily: pick up the guitar and work on some songs; the guitar standing next to the fireplace is difficult for me to pass up. Yet, I still know that music is not my primary field, for I always felt the need to be a "serious artist," a True Artist, and that requires mastery. The desire was always in me, that intention to become really good at something creative. When the person I told you about asked me what my primary purpose in life was, I had to consider this musician side of me, but when I thought about it hard, I could not see myself getting my bearing in

CHAPTER THIRTY

the music world, and performing all the time. Maybe I am too much of an introvert, but I just could not *see* myself doing it.

But there was something that I felt was "my natural field" for sure, that field was drawing and painting. Here I could *see* a future. I had always felt drawing to be my natural métier. I felt, maybe arrogantly so, that I understood drawing naturally and deeply, even though my skills were hardly there to back up that claim. However, I could <u>see</u> myself gaining those skills and becoming good at it; that stood before me clearly, unlike the musician thing. And that is how it played out.

Eventually, explaining art and showing it to many students for many years, both beginning and advanced at the college level, became another advance on my own road to mastery. Even though I already had some track record, it cemented my skill set in place, opening the path to mastery. Even if others saw my work as "masterful," I often knew deep inside that it was not or not yet truly my own, which is what mastery is all about after all. Others would tell me that I was too hard on myself, but I knew what it was supposed to be, and I knew it was not there yet. Ultimately, we were both right. When I revisit some of my earlier work, I see that it is good enough, but I also know that I was right in feeling that there was further to go.

Technique can be learned; it is a known quantity. Mastery is a whole other dimension but cannot exist without the technical core. The reputation of the art college I taught at was based on its emphasis on solid technique, while most university departments were serving up highfalutin modernist approaches to making art.

DRAWING

Over the years I have become absolutely convinced that one of the most effective ways of acquiring proficiency in creating visual imagery is drawing. And I mean with pencil and paper!

The generation that has grown up with the computer and has not known a world without it, has a unique challenge there. They must come to understand that the game-changing technology of the computer, however exciting and amazing, also ushered in a critical cultural climate that questioned all that went before. The computer seemed to displace almost everything in life. The computer got rid of our cameras, our phones, our alarm clocks, our street maps, our encyclopedia, our post mail, our record players, our privacy, our sketchbooks, and our pencils and paper, not to mention canvas and brushes. "Out with it all" seems the be the tenor of our times. We will soon enough come to see it differently.

More than ever, I repeat, more than ever before, we need something to ground us in reality, in our immediate environment, in our being in the world. A basic proficiency that had been accepted and self-evident for centuries, has now come to be seen as obsolete. It is part of the modern mind's narcissism to regard itself as the pinnacle of human achievement. Those with the experience of it, know this is just empty rationalization, opinion at best, not rooted in fact. While drawing with drawing utensils is not the only way of doing things, it is a commonsense approach. There is another dimension to this approach to the great tradition and it was made clear in one of those attic treasures I discovered while rummages around in there. It has to do with attitude.

CHAPTER THIRTY

WAYNE'S WORDS

I have a powerful memory of a university talk given by famous California artist Wayne Thiebaud, which I retrieved from the attic of my mind. It is from the time when I was still a student, and Thiebaud must have been in his sixties. He went on to live to a hundred and one years old, so he must have done something right. Wayne's work is firmly rooted in the realist tradition and thoroughly contemporary as well, showing playful, formalistic inventiveness. I want to remember I. M. Pei's dictum that to innovate you must have roots, and that those roots have to be deep. After the lecture he opened the floor to questions, when a smart aleck student, of which there is always at least one in a university audience, asked Wayne Thiebaud if he did not think that the realist tradition was actually dead by now. The answer he gave was so powerful that it became one of those moments of truth that stands out and kept me on my own path. It was powerful in its simplicity, directness and undeniable truth. Without hesitation he simply and curtly replied, "*I* am doing it!" with an emphasis on the "*I*." In other words, the fact that he was doing it and making a huge success of it showed that it was not dead but very much alive. It was a thoroughly modernist answer to a would-be iconoclast's question; an unapologetic "*I* am doing it!" was enough. No complicated explanations and aesthetic theories needed. I learned from that that part of mastery is knowing when you have enough of it, sufficient to the task. Then you can take a firm stance against inner doubts and outer criticism and say, *I* am doing it, and that *I* am doing it is sufficient proof! In fact, if I do it so well that it makes me well-known, I am giving the lie to all those who say that it is old hat or something. There will always be a sense of discontent with the way things are and have been, as exhibited by the questioner in the audience, but the answer to that is not throwing out the old, but *more mastery*, allowing for a proud stance of "this is who I am!" The masterful artist knows that mastery is never finished, but that one must come to a moment when you know that you have to get on with the work with what you have gathered. That is what it means to be "keepers of the flame." Tending the fire cannot wait until you feel that you are ready, or it will go out in the meantime. At the same time, it demands that you do it effectively.

What is needed is a firm and definite affirmation of one's own natural inclinations, honed and tempered by mastery. Some artists get it early, most tend to get it over time. Modern art education often squashes an artist's original enthusiasm for approaching art in his or her own way. This often leads to giving up on art, no matter how many degrees have been gathered. While some of these theories are a positive challenge to our thinking, they often generate a dismissive stance towards technique and subsequent mastery. This is destructive to the spirit of True Artists. This type of education pushes art making from the body into the head. Keepers of the flame get fuel for the fire from the deeper recesses of their being, which are both in the body and in the mind. Our body has a wisdom all its own and a True Artist engages it.

In the same beaten-up old box where I found the memory of Wayne Thiebaud's lecture in my attic, I recovered a memory from being a student in art college. The modernist iconoclast turmoil had taken possession of many students' minds, and I had started to doubt my own enthusiasms which had brought me amongst them. This attic treasure concerns a conversation with a "modernism-possessed" student. I told him that I aspired to draw like the great (old) masters I admired. His response was a snarky, "Why would you want to do *that*?!" Because the contempt was so powerful, I remember all at once feeling beaten down and that there was something wrong with me for being so behind the times. Thankfully my desire to become proficient at drawing was strong enough to survive and pull me through years of learning, and eventually teaching it. It seemed my desire was not aligned with the ideology of supposedly serious art students. But who could teach me what I wanted to learn? Apparently, drawing in the great master mode was now relegated to the category of being old-fashioned. Perhaps the time spent pursuing my university degrees had made me ignorant of the great advances in art education that had taken place during that time! Or so I thought. Wrongly. To whom could I turn to learn what I still wanted to learn?

Eventually I realized that the master tradition of drawing and painting, truly one of the grandest in world history, was still alive especially in a specialized corner of the art world. It was alive and well with illustrators and animators, those who had to produce and produce, and grab an audience. From them I ultimately learned the most about drawing. And fortuneately, somehow my sense of destiny was strong enough to *also* realize that it was against my deepest instincts to embrace their commercial approach. I could take what they had to offer and use it in the pursuit of my own work. I am glad I had that understanding at the time. Later, I found wonderful teachers who were deeply rooted in the grand tradition while doing their own work and making an impact with their work. So, now I can dust off that attic treasure memory of my encounter with the fellow student and make it a shining one. My love for drawing and my drive to get good at it was what supported me in what felt often like a lonely struggle (only later I realized it was not) towards mastery. Again, it is said that when it comes to the great tradition of art, we should not try to imitate or even emulate the masters but "seek what they sought." I realize that I have always intuitively done just that, long before I heard someone expressing it so beautifully. The problem was that much of the time I thought I was foolish for doing so. As much as I felt out of place amongst the modernist iconoclasts, I also felt out of place with the illustrator and animator crowd, though I retained my deep respect and admiration for their professional prowess and extensive knowledge. I have a special place in my heart for them for it was they who helped me rescue my own sense of what I was to do. I was answering to a different call, but I needed what they had. I realized then that as a True Artist you stand alone, no matter how the world identifies you. Many modernist iconoclasts also had my admiration, even if temperamentally I just never could get behind their fervor in denouncing the grand tradition. This too is why mastery is essential because it gives you solid ground to stand on when evaluating ideologies coming at you from many places in academic life. I have often felt compelled to declare allegiance to one or the other. Therefore, I say that if you find within yourself an inclination to draw, then learn to draw *well*. Then do not stop there but use what you must to deepen your being. Drawing is both an exploration of the world around you and an exploration of yourself. It aligns with the wisdom of the body. Start going through all that supposed junk in your mental attic and find the antiques. I remember a billboard on a freeway in Northern California next to a salvage yard saying, "We buy junk and sell antiques." Your mastery will turn your attic junk into antiques.

CHAPTER THIRTY

The good news is that the practice of drawing is known in all its aspects, the product of many generations of artists sifting all available knowledge and approaches. There is nothing to invent, but there is a great deal to explore and make one's own. First, though, comes learning the basics, and those are simple really. The internet is chockfull of how-to videos dealing with drawing from every conceivable angle, much of it catering to instant results. Do not get attached to any approach, keep moving. Especially if you are of the generation that grew up on comics and anime, make sure to not get stuck there. Both are in essence a simplification and standardization of aspects of classical drawing. Study the classical approach and you get it all. It is not that difficult! Approach it as a serious practice, the way that martial artists practice their kicks, their moves, in a disciplined and regular fashion. Drawing the nude body has always been the standard practice because all the aspects of drawing come into play there.

The high standards for Western style drawing were set during the Renaissance and its aftermath. Everything coming after was a commentary on what was figured out then. Some of this commentary is brilliant and a positive contribution, some of it merely a brazen and often trivial reaction to it or against it.

So, if we are convinced that it is a worthwhile use of our time to pursue a drawing practice, how do we approach it? My recommendation is to grab some paper and a pencil, learn how to sharpen it, and start drawing. Go to a drawing workshop, because a teacher is better than the internet, though there we can learn as well. Start using your whole body in drawing. You will learn that the large, sweeping lines of a drawing, which give the energy to it, are movements of the whole arm, starting from the shoulder, refined by the elbow, and then the wrist, and ultimately the fingers. Our bodies are designed that way. Most people draw with their fingers alone, and some minimal movements of the hands. The computer favors that: just the hand, the fingers too, but only minimal movements, which are ultimately only a small part of the body. Most of us start going are after "effects" because they win applause, but the effects we really want are the result of a consistent drawing practice. Computer programs mimic the effects from the movements of the body while drawing and are therefore not natural. Phenomenology, a branch of philosophy, calls the body engaged in activity "the lived body." Ultimately the affirmation of our True Artist destiny will not come from the dazzling effects we may be able to create on the computer, but from lending ourselves, body and soul, to our work. Let me repeat—body, together with soul. Soul with body. If you are not comfortable with the word "soul," call it "essential nature," or "inner being," or the "spirit of creativity." This is not something nebulous but something real, deep within us. I am planning another book on how to access that "deep within" because that is one of the open secrets of art; available all over the place yet hidden from most of us somehow.

By learning to draw you are shooting down roots which will help you weather the storms you are sure to encounter in your True Artist life. Whenever I am out of sorts or not knowing what to do next or feeling uninspired or at a loss, I continue drawing. I compare it to doing scales on the piano to help the fingers remember where the keys are, as brilliant classical pianist friends have shown me. To call something a "practice" means that it is not some knowledge that you access once, understand, and then have to use for good; it is something you have to keep on doing and doing, making it into a habit.

CHAPTER THIRTY

I used to sketch a lot outside in the world, sitting in coffee shops or traveling. At a certain moment I realized that I had fallen in the habit of just taking photos with my ever-present smart phone camera and was no longer making quick sketches in the little sketchbook I was still carrying with me. "I will work out those photos later on" was the thought, but that seldom happened. Once I became aware of how I had been seduced into some sort of "technological complacency," I quickly returned to the good habit of sketching, and it re-energized the creative spirit. Technology bewitches us and takes us out of ourselves. You can be certain that it has not found its proper assigned place in our existence yet, for when it does, the world will be different and better. Currently it is, in all its dazzling possibilities, more of a disrupter than real progress. For now, it seems intent on taking over our lives, and we must take a stance against it. True Artists must necessarily lead the way to a direct engagement with life. Drawing is the consequential core of that endeavor. Becoming good at drawing will give innumerable advantages. However, as a True Artist, you need to be aware that even becoming a superior draftsman will not make you a True Artist. It will however help in solidifying your position. A lack of ability to draw will undermine you as an artist, especially as a visual artist. At the same time, it also is not the one-in-all answer we are always searching for. As my "secret brotherhood mentor" would say, "Technique does not the artist make, but a lack of technique surely unmakes the artist."

CHAPTER THIRTY-ONE
The Wandering

As said before, this book was not meant to be some step-by-step program guide for finding your destiny, identifying your path. It was always intended to take on the less enviable task of identifying those whom we have called True Artists, who are people of a certain destiny, and deserve their proper place as important parts of their communities. Therefore, the approach we have taken in this book has been more one of a wandering than of proceeding in a straight line to some final destination. This is perfectly in line with the True Artist's life. A wanderer, unlike the purposeful traveler going to a destination, lingers now here, now there and allows him—or herself to be fascinated by things encountered on the way. In our approach to the True Artist's life, we have allowed ourselves the same freedom as the wanderer. Investigating our destiny does not allow for a linear exposé; but requires a path with suggestive hints that are followed up and properly understood. Of course we read the road signs, but we give ourselves the freedom to follow them or take a side path instead. Our instincts, our own sense of direction, may be off and we may suffer because of it, but we have allowed ourselves room for those kinds of mistakes. Andreas-Salome says it so well, when she says that it is not just our strengths that produce good work, but

CHAPTER THIRTY-ONE

our frailties as well. Wandering is not purposeless, it is not a meandering, it is goal-oriented but in a deeper organic way. Its sense of destination lies elsewhere, like an underground river flowing beneath the surface, unseen, yet purposeful. Wandering is a way of being in the world, a creative way of life for the True Artist.

J. R. R. Tolkien is most well-known for his *The Lord of the Rings* and *The Hobbit,* but he was much more than a writer of mythological fairy tales. He was a serious scholar and professor of Middle and Old English at Oxford University in England. Having a natural linguistic talent, he mastered Greek and Latin (still a staple of an arts education at that time), he also mastered an old language like Gothic (which was no longer spoken, unlike Latin and Greek) and contemporary Finnish as well. All this gave him a core proficiency around which he would build his mastery. He grouped several of his natural inclinations into this core proficiency, engaging his poetic gifts as well as his fertile imagination, which set him to invent his own language as seen in his *The Lord of the Rings*. In this he shows his True Artist nature, but there is more than that in his approach to life that spells True Artist throughout. Somehow, he landed in the trenches of the first World War as a British soldier in France during the Somme offensive, one of the most brutal and decisive battles of that or any war. Right after this active combat experience, which sent him to a military hospital, he set out to write early versions of the stories for which he would become so well-known. These writings have not been published but became the basis of much that was to follow. He eventually landed back at Oxford University in England, where he had gotten his degree, but now as a professor, becoming what is known as an "Oxford don," part of a very elite and serious academic faculty circle. Though a valued professor, he seems not to have been a standout faculty member, having few academic publications to his name in a world where those were and are the currency of distinction. The Oxford don status was not an easy fit for him, though he seemed to have enjoyed being in the company of serious scholars. These serious men are said to have frowned upon what must to them have seemed like silly stories their colleague was putting out, if they even knew of their existence at all. Yet his artistic output, in True Artist fashion, spoke of great mastery built out from a solid core of proficiency. It consisted of his different interests put in service of a visionary imagination. We can see his extensive knowledge of languages coming together with his deep interest in and knowledge of mythology; also, his imaginal capacities meeting up with his all-too-real trench warfare experiences, and it is well to remember that World War I trench warfare was exceptionally savage. What he became world-renowned for was actually just a part of a much wider and larger project of his life. While his serious colleagues may have scornfully wondered why their esteemed colleague was occupying his time with childlike imaginary tales, he was creating work that spoke to future generations. Many of his notebooks and writings are still left unpublished, stored in a garage left for one of his sons to go through. These are "attic treasures" if ever there were any.

Does all this not speak of the True Artist trajectory? It is wonderful getting to know about his life, seeing that he had that core proficiency in an area of natural interest and inclination, around which a natural mastery grew. I also felt close to him when I read that he did not succumb to the trap of being part of a prestigious faculty, though he was a dedicated teacher. Not that I compare Oxford with where I taught, nonetheless, the issues remain the same for all.

CHAPTER THIRTY-ONE

Additionally, I was delighted to know that he too held on to his notebooks and stored them and no less in a garage, which is where most of my own notebooks are now too, after moving into a new house.

His writings include gems of insights and beautiful poetic lines that go to the heart of the matter of the True Artist destiny. Here is a sample of a few I particularly like in the context of this book:

> "All that is gold does not glitter,
> Not all those who wander are lost;
> The old that is strong does not wither,
> Deep roots are not reached by the frost."

This encapsulates the subject matter of this book. Here Tolkien first gives us a clever and meaningful reversal of the common saying "all that glitters is not gold," and remakes it into "all that is gold does not glitter." It is his way of saying that the ingredients of an unfolding destiny are not necessarily glittering things inspiring awe, but simple, commonplace things. These turn out the be the real gold, but they do not announce themselves as such; they are not brightly shining things. The common life experiences of the True Artist are as valid as anything as the basic ingredients for their art. Again, we land in the comparison with the alchemist's pursuits. The real ingredients for the glittering things are the raw materials of life; these are our base materials, the prima materia. What is golden in us, does not announce itself necessarily by some brilliance shining through. Tolkien also says here, in the way of a poet, that there are those whose wandering is a deep search, and that they are not necessarily lost; theirs is not a purposeless meandering. Some are inner wanderers, others outer wanderers, but the endeavor is the same. It speaks of a way of being open to the many experiences that life brings and a willingness to work with them. There is no GPS for wanderers. Mapping out the road to a destination is not possible, because the destination is not known. Other than the signs coming from an awareness of an unfolding destiny, there are no markers. Wandering is a way of advancing on a path that will show its purpose only when looking back over the ground covered. All adventures along the way, all treasures from our mental attic, contribute to the significance of the journey and also of the arriving. On the way, the wanderer may get sidetracked, distracted, or detoured, but the port of call remains in place, for that is where the flow deep inside is heading. Outer adversities cannot assail the depths where true destiny resides. Says Tolkien, "Deep roots are not reached by the frost." Here he says that our destiny is not destroyed by adversity on the way, which he calls "frost" here, for it cannot reach deep enough, not deep enough into us. These are the deep roots architect I. M. Pei mentioned as well, and he spoke of them as the prerequisite for innovation.

One last note on Tolkien, a very exceptional one at that. Apparently, the name Tolkien comes from his German ancestors and derives from Toll-kühn, meaning "foolishly brave," or "stupidly clever."[1] J.R.R.'s life seems to speak of just that kind of attitude. So too seems the life project of the True Artist—foolishly brave.

---

1   David Doughan MBE:" J. R. R. Tolkien, a biographical sketch." The Tolkien Society.org

Afterword

Once I finished the book I immediately saw that there is a whole new book waiting to be written; a book in which all the aspects of the subject that could not find a place in the book; those that had to be taken out not to overload the central subject with too many side issues. I tend to go off course in that way. I repeat myself, and that is part of the wandering. In this book, the main point was to identify what we have called the True Artist destiny. We made sure that we used "true" in the way that it is used in the way we speak of "true" love. Here "true" means that it connects with the deepest and most natural creative impulses in us, those the "frost" of which Tolkien speaks cannot reach. We made clear that this distinction is necessary because the True Artist's identity has become submerged in a tidal wave of often well-meaning attempts to call anyone who shows some creativity an "artist." It bears repeating, because our times seem obsessed with this. In this they show that we regard "being an artist" as a very desirable thing to be. Why this is so tells us a lot about the psychology of modern men and women, but a further investigation of that would have to go into that book, waiting to be written. From my perspective it seems to point to some sense of lack in the life of the modern person.

For the True Artist, being an artist is not just something to be desired, but a necessity. For the True Artist, it is not a career choice but a destiny; destiny being something that must be followed, rather than pursued. Though the early phases of destiny unfolding often—and necessarily—take the form of a pursuit, as destiny becomes clear in the way we begin to shape our life and begin to "follow" rather than pursue that which is taking shape.

We looked at how destiny first announces itself only vaguely and then in ever clearer intimations which eventually start making an intelligible whole. We came to realize the layout of what we are meant to be gradually, guided by some inner necessity, and that it is a life-long journey. The inner necessity is not always felt as a welcome guest because it demands that we go our own way when all others seem to be doing "the sensible thing." It bears repeating that for a very few, clarity comes early, but for most it only slowly unfolds. We may have times that we think we have gained some clarity, only to see it fade again. Such is the nature and character of destiny.

Since the unfolding of destiny is at first a sketchy enterprise at best, I have tried to approach the subject in a way that leaves the subject open for readers to find their own way. I did this by looking at my own personal experiences, my so-called "mental attic pieces," and the stories of the lives of others who crossed my path in significant ways. In telling these experiences, I have pointed out how things somehow start to "happen" and point the way, once we are decidedly on the path; then we start to follow, rather than pursue. These experiences also show that while our own lives may not be as dramatic or glamorous as presented in grand biographies of famous artists, we all have the necessary elements for a meaningful unfolding. I also brought in some of the art historical greats, the ones about whom biographies are written, to show what their lives had to teach me and have to teach us. So, while insisting on personal exploration, in the spirit of the book, I had to leave things open for readers to find their own way. It is easy (and fun) to get lost in biographies of great artists written by great writers (for whom that is *their* artistry), but ultimately what counts is our own lives. We have nothing else. The guidance I can provide is always meant as prods to move us along on the path that is often lonely and always challenging, in the way I received those prods myself from others. Above all then, this book is meant to be a companion on the long, exciting, but complicated journey.

The True Artist is someone who has something to say and feels compelled to say it to shine a light on the present in some way, directly or indirectly. That means that as a child of his and her time, the True Artist has a sense of the essential spirit of the present moment in history and is "tuned in" in some way and has the wherewithal (mastery) to state his or her case. True Artists feel an inner push, a need really, to deal with their own times in some way, giving it form, by means of their own life experiences. True Artists, we realize, arise in every period, in every society, in every circumstance, and necessarily deal with the situation they find themselves in. Our current times are especially challenging since they are in a continual flux. Yet, it is the True Artist who finds things that are underneath this flux. This may position him or her squarely in their own times or in opposition to them, but it always involves a search for just the right way to say things and the proper format to tell them in. Again, this comes down to the pursuit of "mastery" which is the pursuit of a lifetime. It is the one constant in the True Artist's life, and there is no True Artist life without it. Since mastery is not readily understood, I have tried to give it definition, based on many years of teaching experience and personal struggle. It needs to be understood just right to embrace it fully and joyfully. I have indicated steps to mastery based on the insights of many great teachers and from my own personal perspective. However it is done, it cannot be ignored.

The True Artist knows that having good ideas and having something to say are not the same thing. Though good ideas are naturally a part of all good work, the True Artist tunes into that something underlying the "good ideas." It is said that good ideas are "in the air" and they need to be grasped by someone or else they disappear. Clever ideas, an off shoot of good ideas, are often given too much prominence. However, they can also be that little extra that enlivens the whole, so I do not dismiss them. They are the spices thrown into a dish to excite the palate. They can never be the main course so to speak, and they certainly should not take over the whole dish. They are the 'discord colors' a painter uses to enliven the composition. Discord colors lie outside the formal color harmonies being pursued and do not really fit with the harmonic scheme, but in just the right amount give that extra burst of energy that makes a work exciting. This is all part of mastery, which allows us to manage the often conflicting and apparently contradictory forces that we see at play all around us, as well as within ourselves.

The pursuit of mastery in and of itself is a bulwark against the anti-cultural impulses which always threaten to disembowel culture. They are, and always have been, at play within and without; sometimes more so, sometimes less so. They are very much in evidence in our times, and by their very nature, and because of the amplification allowed by technology, louder, more insistent, and garnering much attention. The True Artist knows that destruction comes easy, creation not so much. Alchemy has something to tell us about that. We looked at the alchemist's laboratory where tending the flame, keeping the fire always burning at just the right temperature, was primary. Alchemy, because it was such a truly global phenomenon, must have something to tell us about what happens in all societies. It tells me that by keeping the flame properly tended that the negatives will be incorporated and given a proper place among the positives. This never precludes being critical of one's own time, for that is a natural component of the work, but it does preclude the anti-cultural impulses that are merely destructive. The True Artist remains in touch with the directive to always be "a keeper of the flame."

The book is dedicated to all those who know that destiny is calling and are fighting the fight to keep that call alive and respond to what they know are their best impulses. You, dear reader, are one of the ones that our times and our society needs and needs badly. We have more than enough entertainment, more than enough spectacle, but little true nourishment. Yours is the endeavor of meaning, and in this, you, the True Artist are an "essential worker." You who work on the deeper structures of the human spirit are needed. You who tend the roots of the surface phenomena are essential. It has been my desire to reach out to you whom I call in this book—in a cheerful way—members of the secret brotherhood. We do not know each other, yet in a special way we do.

www.ingramcontent.com/pod-product-compliance
Lightning Source LLC
Chambersburg PA
CBHW011403210526
45464CB00008B/3030